SQUADRONS!

No. 6

THE SUPERMARINE
SPITFIRE MK. VII

PHIL H. LISTEMANN

ISBN: 978-2918590-45-3

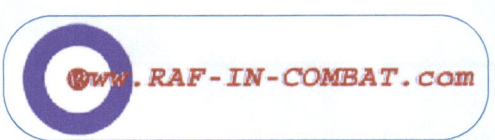

Copyright

© 2014 Philedition - Phil Listemann
revised - Dec.2018

Colour profiles: Gaetan Marie/Bravo Bravo Aviation

All right reserved. No part of this book may be reproduced, stored in a retrieval system or transmitted in any form by any means, electronic, mechanical, photocopying, recording or otherwise, without prior permission of the author.

Contributors & Acknowledgments:
Peter Arnold, André Bar, Chris Goss, Drew Harrison, Jiri Rajlich, Paul Sortehaug, Andrew Thomas, Chris Thomas

GLOSSARY OF TERMS

PERSONEL :

(AUS)/RAF: Australian serving in the RAF
(BEL)/RAF: Belgian serving in the RAF
(CAN)/RAF: Canadian serving in the RAF
(CZ)/RAF: Czechoslovak serving in the RAF
(NFL)/RAF: Newfoundlander serving in the RAF
(NL)/RAF: Dutch serving in the RAF
(NZ)/RAF: New Zealander serving in the RAF
(POL)/RAF: Pole serving in the RAF
(SR)/RAF: Rhodesian serving in the RAF
(SA)/RAF: South African serving in the RAF
(US)/RAF - RCAF : American serving in the RAF or RCAF

RANKS

G/C : Group Captain
W/C : Wing Commander
S/L : Squadron Leader
F/L : Flight Lieutenant
F/O : Flying Officer
P/O : Pilot Officer
W/O : Warrant Officer
F/Sgt : Flight Sergeant
Sgt : Sergeant
Cpl : Corporal
LAC : Leading Aircraftman

OTHER

ATA: Air Transport Auxiliary
CO : Commander
DFC : Distinguished Flying Cross
DFM : Distinguished Flying Medal
DSO : Distinguished Service Order
Eva. : Evaded
ORB : Operational Record Book
OTU : Operational Training Unit
PoW : Prisoner of War
PAF: Polish Air Force
RAF : Royal Air Force
RAAF : Royal Australian Air Force
RCAF : Royal Canadian Air Force
RNZAF : Royal New Zealand Air Force
SAAF : South African Air Force
s/d: Shot down
Sqn : Squadron
† : Killed

CODENAMES - OFFENSIVE OPERATIONS - FIGHTER COMMAND

CIRCUS:
Bombers heavily escorted by fighters, the purpose being to bring enemy fighters into combat.

RAMROD:
Bombers escorted by fighters, the primary aim being to destroy a target.

RANGER:
Large formation freelance intrusion over enemy territory with aim of wearing down enemy fighters.

RHUBARD:
Freelance fighter sortie against targets of opportunity.

ROADSTEAD:
Dive bombing and low level attacks on enemy ships at sea or in harbour

RODEO:
A fighter sweep without bombers.

SWEEP:
An offensive flight by fighters designed to draw up and clear the enemy from the sky.

THE SPITFIRE MK VII

Despite following closely after the previous Mark, the VI (see SQUADRONS! No.1), the VII was very different even though both were designed to fulfil the same high altitude interception role. Externally the VII can be mainly distinguished from the VI by its retractable tail wheel. Less obvious was the reduction of the aileron span and a double-glazed sliding hood. The engine was also different as the VII could have a Merlin 61, 64 or 71 installed. Most, however, were equipped with the 1,710 hp Merlin 64.

With the Mk.VII, Supermarine had tried to redesign the Spitfire. Even if the early models had the original shape fin and rudder, this was later superseded by the broad-chord rudder with pointed tip. The armament remained the same incorporated in the 'C' wing with extended tips and reduced span ailerons. Two fuel tanks of 14 gallons each were installed in the leading edge and the cooling system was also redesigned to include radiator air scoops under each wing.

The Mk.VII was, as a result, 15% heavier than a Mk.V or a Mk.VI but, despite this, was 10% faster with a top speed exceeding 400mph.

Spitfire AB450 was the first aircraft to be converted to Mk.VII standard and was completed in July 1942. 140 others followed with deliveries ending in May 1944. The bulk were delivered in 1943 with 74 Mk.VIIs taken on charge. The breakdown of the deliveries is as follow:

1942: BS121, BS142, BS229, BS253, EN178, EN192, EN285, EN297 (8)
1943: EN310, EN457, EN465, EN470, EN474, EN477, EN494-497, EN499, EN505, EN506, EN509, EN511, EN512, MB761-MB769, MB806, MB808, MB820-MB828, MB912-MB916, MB929-MB931, MD100-MD116, MD118-MD120, MD127 (65)
1944: MB883-MB887, MB932-MB935, MD117, MD121-MD126, MD128-MD146, MD159-MD190 (67).

All of the Mk.VIIs were, like the Mk.VI, off-shoots of the Mk.V production line. Four Fighter Command squadrons used the Mk.VII in operations - Nos.124, 131, 154 and 616. No. 154 Squadron used the Mk.VII for a very short time and only as interim equipment. This mark completed about 6,600 sorties and 24 aerial confirmed and probable claims were made. In comparing those figures with the ones of the Mk.VI used in the same role, they appear to be very similar but the losses of the Mk.VII units were much lower as 89 of the 141 built were still in the RAF inventory by VE-Day. Actually this comparison does not really prove any superiority of the Mk.VII over the Mk.VI as such as the Mk.VII probably came too late to play any major role in the Fighter Command missions. Relegated to high altitude defensive operations at first in 1943, only a few successful interceptions were made as the Luftwaffe, at the time, was not presenting a real threat. The Mk.IX had been introduced into service at the same time and, with its similar performance, the Mk.VII did not represent a real advantage. By Spring 1944, the Mk.VII switched to more conventional operations (*Rodeo* and *Ramrod*) and some Mk.VII were even retrofitted with shorter 'classic' wings painted with a conventional Day Fighter Scheme. As with the Mk.VI, some Mk.VIIs found a new role with the Meteorological units but in small numbers. Generally speaking the Mk.VII was not widely used in its original high altitude role so this probably explains the lower loss rate sustained by the Mk.VII units over the Mk.VI (about 110 of 140 produced being still listed in the inventory when the type from withdrawn from the front-line units). The global impact of the Mk.VII on the wartime career of the Spitfire was, as for the Mk.VI, negligible. By early 1945 most of the remaining aircraft were waiting their fate in the MUs – many with low airframe time - and some were issued to training units to fulfil this non-glorious role for a couple of months. This situation continued a while after the war but the type was eventually

Side view of BS142, the second production Spitfire Mk.VII. Delivered in September 1942, it was first issued to the High Altitude Flight at Northolt before serving with 124 Sqn when the flight was absorbed by this squadron. Damaged in an accident in August 1943, on return from an interception, it was not repaired and its fuselage became an instructional airframe in December. Note that BS142 has been painted with the standard Day Fighter camouflage scheme. *(P. Arnold's collection)*

AB450 was built as an Mk.V before being converted as the prototype of the Spitfire Mk.VII (seen here unarmed). It is seen after having been repainted with PR Blue upper surfaces and Deep Sky undersides. This scheme was eventually tested at 124 Sqn in January 1943 before returning to Boscombe Down for further trials the following month. It was eventually struck off charge in June 1944. The trials at 124 were conclusive as the camouflage was adopted for the Mk.VII from 7 June 1943 onwards. *(Peter Arnold's collection)*

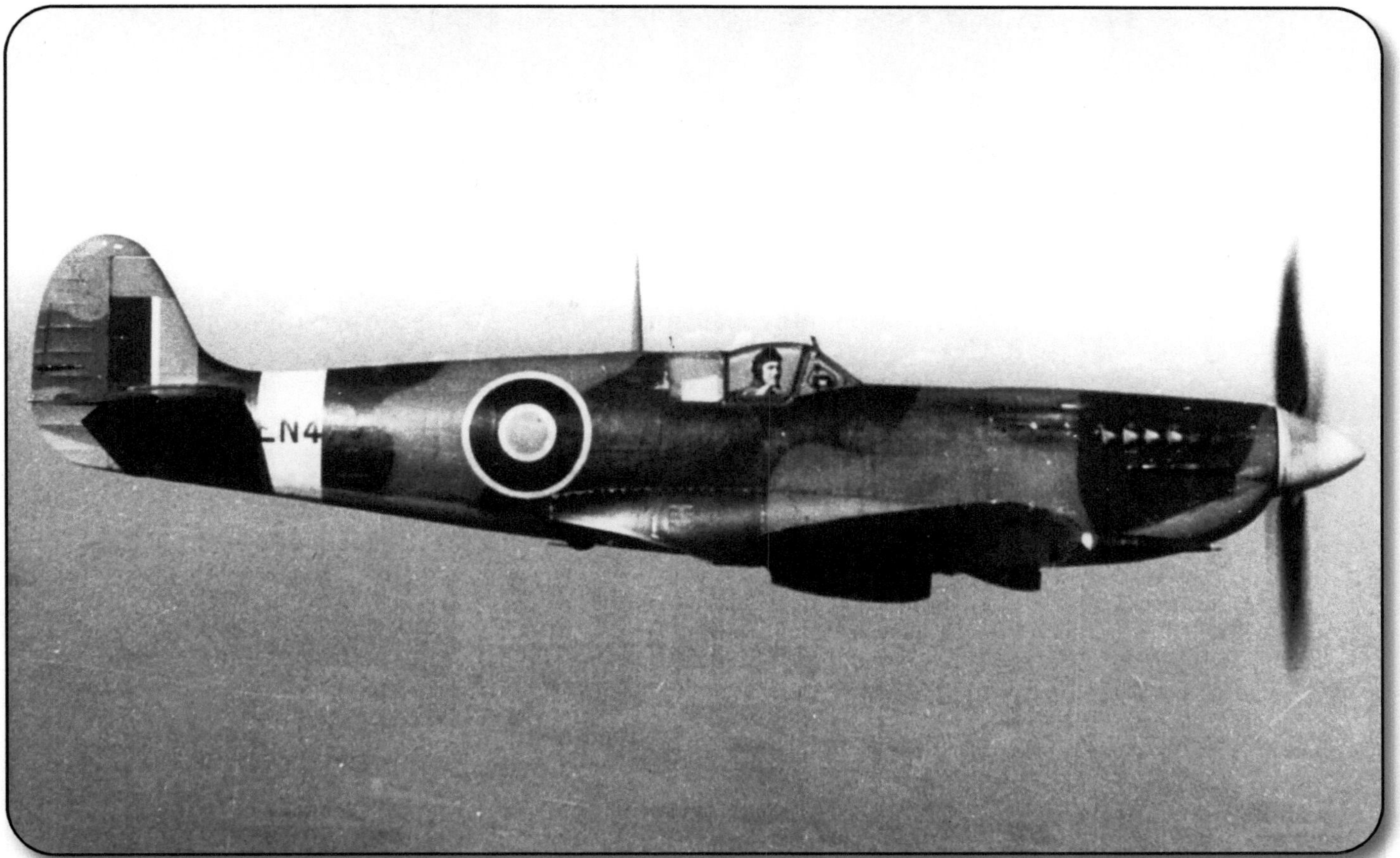

Above, EN474, during a test flight in March 1943, before being handed over to the USAAF the following month. It survived the war.
Below, MD124 was taken on charge at 39 MU on 6 January 1944 and therefore was painted with the new camouflage introduced in June 1943. Note the tail and rudder with the broad-chord rudder and pointed tip. MD124 was used operationally by 131 Sqn and ended its career with meteorological work until November 1945.

March 1943
July 1944

Victories - confirmed or probable claims: 11

First operational sortie: 04.03.43
Last operational sortie: 18.07.44

Number of sorties: ca. 3,150
Total aircraft written-off: 4
Aircraft lost on operations: 2
Aircraft lost in accidents: 2

Squadron code letters:
ON

COMMANDING OFFICERS

S/L James C. Nelson	RAF No. 100525	(US)/RAF	...	23.06.43
S/L Thomas Balmforth	RAF No. 41363	RAF	23.06.43	...

SQUADRON USAGE

No. 124 Squadron was the first to introduce the Mk.VII in combat. This unit was familiar with high altitude Spitfires, being equipped with the Mk.VI since July 1942, but had had no spectacular success nor catastrophic losses (unlike No. 616 Squadron which suffered heavy losses for little return). Actually, 124 was already using the Mk.VII when the first Mk.VII were officially issued to the squadron. It had absorbed the S.S. Flight a couple of weeks previous. It had been flying a several high altitude marks - the Mk.VI, Mk.IX and, of course, the Mk.VII (BS121, BS142 and EN285). The squadron was under the command of a former Eagle Squadron fighter pilot, S/L Nelson, when the first Mk.VII arrived in the first days of March. No. 124 was based at Croughton, north of Oxford, at that time and was carrying out defensive duties only the personnel of the former SS Flight on strength. The main body of the

Left, Jimmy Nelson took over the squadron in December 1942. An American from Colorado, he served with No. 133 (Eagle) Squadron between September 1941 and September 1942. He elected not to transfer to the USAAF and continued to serve in the RAF. When he left 124, he served as a test pilot and was victim of a serious accident on 23 August 1944 while test flying a Mosquito XVI. He never totally recovered and was eventually medically discharged in April 1945.
He was replaced by Tommy Balmforth who had previously commanded 124 before J.C. Nelson. He joined the RAF in October 1938 and when war broke out he was tasked to ferry aircraft between RAF stations. This task led him to ferry Hurricanes in the Middle East in June 1940. His travel was stopped at Malta and was attached to the Fighter Flight which was raised into No. 261 Squadron in August. In January 1941 he was however evacuated to the UK due to ill health. He joined 124 Squadron in September 1941 and was awarded the DFC in May 1942. He was rested in January 1943 but would return in June to lead the squadron again until September 1944, this time to fly Spitfire Mk VIIs. In October 1944 he became Wing Leader at Manston, a position he left in December 1944. He was made Companion of the DSO in April 1945.

F/Sgt Eric "Chunky" Phelps who plunged into the Channel while on patrol on 14 May 1943. He is seen here in Spitfire VI BR329/ON-R at the time No. 124 Squadron was flying on that type. He had joined 124 in March 1942.
(Phelps' family)

unit was participating in Exercise *Spartan*. Therefore, it was only called upon to intercept intruders. It is in this role that 124 recorded its first sortie with a Mk.VII when F/O Oliver Willis took off in EN285 at 9.05 to intercept an intruder. He returned 45 minutes later with nothing to report. In March, the squadron did not carry out many sorties, only the ex-SS Flight being operational, as the squadron moved to Duxford first and then to North Weald on the 12th March where the transition to the Mk.VII began. Only 27 sorties were recorded, 12 being flown with the Mk.VII, the rest with the Mk.VI and the two Mk.IXs (BS271 and BS273). That month, other Mk.VIIs trickled in (EN310 and EN457). Activity remained low in April with the squadron continuing to fly various marks including the Mk.V now. Mk.VII deliveries remained slow with only EN496 arriving in the middle of the month. On the 28th instructions were received to send a detachment to Colerne with three Mk.VIIs (BS142, EN457, EN497), and four pilots - Flying Officers Willis and Wilson and Sergeants Wise and Yeardley.
Still flying both Mk.VI and Mk.VII, even as the number of Mk.VIs diminished during May, the squadron was only called upon to carry out uneventful patrols and scrambles. On the 14th, however, during a patrol, the squadron lost its first Mk.VII. In the evening, two Mk.VIIs, flown by F/Sgt 'Chunky' Phelps and Sgt Landsdown, were ordered to patrol Horshal at 15,000 feet. The section carried out the patrol at the planned altitude between Isle of Wright and Beachy Head and, after completing this twice, they were told to open up and climb to 32,000 feet on a vector 090. When they reached 32,000 feet Green 1 (F/Sgt Phelps) informed the controller he had gone into a steep dive. Green 2 (Sgt Landsdown) followed him in this dive and reached a speed well over 400mph. Phelps was able to regain control of his aircraft and pulled out of the dive. Things seemed to return back to normal and two more vectors were received. Green 2 was asked to take the lead and return to 32,000 feet. He flew past his No.1, waggled his wings and commenced to climb. However, upon reaching 32,000 feet, Phelps was absent and after a little while Landsdown vectored to base. The latter plunged into the Channel 20 miles east of Deal at about 20.50 and his body was never recovered. An investigation concluded that the possible reason for this accident could have been a failure of the oxygen equipment. This first fatal loss was quickly compensated for as, the following day, F/O Oliver Willis of the Colerne detachment claimed a Fw190 destroyed. This was the first success for the Mk.VII. Leading a section, F/O Willis and Sgt Webberley had scrambled at 12.40 to intercept bandits heading for Start Point. When in the vicinity of Newton Abbot at 23,000 feet, a condensation trail was seen climbing fast. The two Spitfires climbed to 36,000 feet, turned behind the enemy aircraft, and continued the climb to 38,000 feet. The Germans were now heading south and the Spitfires turned to cut them off, crossing the east coast off Plymouth at 39,000 feet. The trails were then seen diving fast. F/O Willis dived to 19,000 feet and closed to 400 yards behind two now identified Fw190s. Willis opened fire and saw strikes and flashes around the cockpit and wing roots. The other Fw190 was able to escape in a steep dive while Willis was watching pieces of his victim going down and the pilot baling out. The victim was actually a Bf109G-4 of 4. (F)/123 flown by *Leutnant* Wilhelm Marcks. Later, in the afternoon, another patrol led by F/Sgt Wise (from North Weald) spotted two Bf109s but they were too far away and were not engaged. As far as the Mk.VII was concerned nothing else of interest happened for the rest of the month. The squadron, including the Colerne detachment, had carried out more than 100 sorties with the Mk.VII.
The Spitfire Mk.VII continued to arrive slowly on the squadron which obliged 124 to keep some Mk.VIs on strength for training purposes. Early in June, MB808, MB820 and MB821 were taken on charge. In the first fortnight, only scrambles were carried out. W/O Nowell shot down a Bf109 on one such early morning scramble. It was not the first success for Garry Nowell, who had previously served with 87 and 32 Squadrons as an NCO, as he had already claimed 14 victories confirmed or probable and had received the DFM and Bar. The next day, Nowell had the opportunity to talk with the German pilot, asking many technical questions regarding high altitude flying. The following day, the American CO left the squadron and was replaced by S/L Thomas Balmforth who had led 124 the previous year when the unit was flying the Mk VI (see SQUADRONS! No.1). Scrambles continued until the end of the month but not without incident as F/O Willis had to make a forced-landing on take-off on the 22nd. Thanks to his skill he managed it without a lot of damage to his Spitfire (MB821) and the aircraft was later repaired. Later that month, Nowell became probably the pilot of the month when he shot down an Fw190 on the 27th. He had taken off with F/Sgt Wise to intercept an incoming raid and the section was given several vectors which brought them at 30,000 feet east of Foreland. Two enemy aircraft were seen to port flying in line abreast at 26,000 feet. The section attacked but the Germans saw them and jettisoned their central auxiliary fuel tanks. With a higher speed, the Nowell was able to close to within 150 yards of one of the FW190s. He fired a two second burst and saw the aircraft falling in flames. F/Sgt Wise fired at the second Fw190 from 500 yards but saw no results. It was Nowell's 16th claim and the victim was another reconnaissance Bf109 of the 5(F)./123 time flown by *Feldwebel* Heinz Sieker. It was really a month to remember for Nowell who received notification of his commission two days later.
Even though 140 sorties (scrambles and patrols) were carried out in July, the month was uneventful. While based at North Weald during the summer, the squadron sent detachments to Colerne, Exeter, Bisley and Fairwood Common but nothing really happened during these months. Despite many scrambles and high altitude patrols, only one Bf109 was caught on 16 August by F/O B. Brooks off the Isle of Wight. To keep the squadron active, four aircraft, led by the CO, participated in a *Ramrod* mission on the 30th. The squadron acted as top cover, at 25,000 feet, for the North Weald Wing which had been charged to escort Mitchells attacking St-Omer. September was another quiet month but 124 participated in more *Ramrod* missions. These were always on a small scale with

> Combat report:
> O.E Willis, 15 May 1943, first Mk.VII confirmed claim

Personal
for Perring

SECRET F.C.

FINAL REPORT – DAY DEFENSIVE COMBAT – 124 (BARODA) SQUADRON (FORM "F")   IN43/C11/4

DATE	(A)	15th May 1943
UNIT	(B)	2 a/c 124 (Baroda) Squadron
TYPE AND MARK OF AIRCRAFT	(C)	SPITFIRES VII.
TIME ATTACK WAS DELIVERED	(D)	1310 hours
PLACE OF ATTACK	(E)	55/60 miles S.W. of Start Point.
WEATHER	(F)	No cloud. Thick sea haze.
OUR CASUALTIES – AIRCRAFT	(G)	Nil
OUR CASUALTIES – PERSONNEL	(H)	Nil
ENEMY CASUALTIES IN AIR COMBAT	(J)	One FW 190 DESTROYED by F/O WILLIS.

GENERAL

2 a/c 124 Squadron were scrambled from Exeter at 1235 hrs. to intercept bandits heading for Start Point. When at 23,000 ft. in the vicinity of Newton Abbot, our pilots saw two parallel vapour trails climbing fast and approaching from the S.E. Just before reaching the coast two objects were seen (on account of the trails which they caused) to fall from the enemy aircraft. The trails crossed the coast near Dartmouth and made a wide sweep over Dartmoor, with our aircraft approximately ten miles behind. When the trails turned south recrossing the coast east of Plymouth at approximately 38,000 feet, our aircraft, which had reached 39,000 feet, turned to cut them off and shortened the range to six miles. On recrossing the coast, the enemy aircraft began to dive very fast heading due south. Some 55/60 miles S.W. of Start Point F/O WILLIS, who had dived down to 19,000 feet, approached within 400 yards of the two FW 190s, which were flying side by side separated by about 150 yards. F/O WILLIS' No.2 (SGT. WIBBERLEY) was approximately ½ mile behind him, but was not able to catch him up as they were flying at maximum speed. The enemy aircraft did not seem to know they were being chased. F/O WILLIS fired two bursts of several seconds from dead astern from 400 yards closing to 300 yards and saw strikes around fuselage and wing roots. The enemy aircraft skidded, disappearing from view below the nose of our aircraft. The other enemy aircraft immediately dived steeply away and was lost from view in the haze. Our pilot turned to follow the enemy aircraft which he had engaged, and saw a parachute open several thousand feet below and pieces of aircraft hurtling down to the sea. Our pilot gave Mayday for the bandit, whom he last saw in the sea, but no dinghy was visible. Our aircraft landed back at Exeter 1415 hrs.

Controller: F/O Holly.
Rounds fired: 90 from each cannon.
Weather: No cloud. Thick sea haze.
Cine guns: Not fitted to F/O WILLIS' machine.
CLAIM: One FW 190 DESTROYED by F/O WILLIS (124).

for Squadron Intelligence Officer
124 (Baroda) Squadron

PERSONAL REPORT relative to the above.

I was scrambled to intercept two bandits reported heading for Start Point at 1235 hrs. 15 May/43. At 1310 hours, when approximately 60 miles S.W. of Start Point, I opened fire on one of the e/a from astern at 400 yds range, seeing strikes on fuselage and wing roots. The enemy aircraft was then lost from view, but I turned to re-engage and saw a parachute open and pieces of aircraft falling down to the sea. I claim this e/a as one FW 190 destroyed.

F/O O. WILLIS
124 (Baroda) Squadron.

New Zealander Paul Haywood, left, flew high altitude Spitfires almost exclusively - the Mk.VI and Mk.VII. He completed a tour with 124 Squadron between May 1942 and September 1944. He became a Flight commander in March 1943. He survived the war.

Right, Albert M. Charlesworth arrived on the Squadron in October 1943 for a second tour. He became a Flight commander in July during the last days of the Mk.VII. He continued to serve the squadron until the end of the war. He had started his first tour in August 1941 with 118 Sqn followed by a posting to No.602 and No.32 Squadrons in North Africa.

only four aircraft generally being dispatched. However, with routine operations still being carried out, the number of sorties increased for the month. It was during one of these routine flights that the squadron claimed its fifth victory – a Bf109 on the 9th - Patrolling at 26,000 feet, in the vicinity of the Isle of Wight, F/O Philipps and P/O Barritt were given several vectors to reach one aircraft approaching at from Cherbourg at 31,000 feet. Soon, vapour trials were seen and chase was on. The section was able to close to 200 yards and then closer again - F/O Philipps fired at it from 50 yards. Hits were seen on the port wing roots and cockpit and the aircraft was seen to flick over and spin before it hit the sea and disappeared.

On 2 October, the squadron carried out eight patrols and one scramble. At 1645, the third last patrol of the day was flown by F/Sgts Kelly and Nelson who were soon called to intercept two Fw190s flying at the Spitfires' altitude of 29,000 feet. The Germans were spotted about 30 miles SSW of the Isle of Wight and did not see the Spitfires until they had closed to about 1,000 yards. They reacted by diving sharply away but Kelly managed to get close enough to fire a short burst from about 400 yards. No hits were seen but he followed the Fw190 down which pulled away in the dive. Kelly's air speed indicator registered over 500 mph! He started to pull out of the dive at 10,000 feet and, careful to avoid over-stressing the airframe, he eventually levelled out at 1,000 feet. At once he tried to find the enemy aircraft but no trace of it could be found. As the enemy was still diving when Kelly began to ease out of his dive, he concluded that the German pilot had left his pull out too late and crashed into the sea. Kelly therefore claimed it as being a probable victory. The day wasn't over for 124 as two Spitfires were vectored to intercept two more Fw190s at mid-channel between Boulogne and Dungeness during the last patrol of the day. The two pilots, F/L P. Haywood and F/Sgt M.J. Blanch, failed to find them as they disappeared into the dusk at 23,000 feet. The squadron continued to patrol over the next few days without anything to report and the weather prevented any flying between the 10th and the 12th. On the 13th, some local flying resumed but one Mk.VII was lost in an accident during a practice flight after an engine failure at 2,000 feet. The pilot, F/Sgt Duckett, made a forced-landing. The aircraft was later declared un-repairable. Operational flying resumed on the 15th. Two days later the squadron was again successful in shooting down an Fw190. Flight Sergeant A.D. Yeardley and Sgt G.R. Clarke chased three Fw190s and caught one of them at 28,000 feet. The Fw190 tried to return to France but Yeadley fired several short bursts until his cannons jammed. It was enough, however, as he noticed the German pilot bailing out. The rest of October was uneventful except for one unsuccessful interception on the 24th. There was no operational flying after the 26th owing to the bad weather.

November and December 1943 were rather uneventful with mainly scrambles and patrols carried out. The weather in those months affected a lot of the operations but the squadron was not unique in encountering this problem. The pilots of 124 participated in 18 *Ramrods* (seven in November and eleven in December) over this period and usually acted as the top cover of the fighter escort flying at around 27,000 feet. Despite those escorts, the squadron didn't encounter the enemy as much as it would have liked. Only the second *Ramrod* on 20 December - escort of American Marauders to St-Omer – provided an opportunity but without success. Squadron Leader Bamforth fired an ineffectual burst at one Fw190 and F/L Kilburn could not put himself in a good enough position to fire a single burst at another Fw190. Lack of luck didn't help either on the 24th when two Mk.VIIs took off (F/L P. Haywood and F/O W.J. Hibbert) to intercept two enemy aircraft which turned for home when they saw the Spitfires approaching. 1943 ended with an uneventful scramble (P/O G.L. Nowell and F/Sgt D.W. Lansdown) closing a year which saw the squadron completing over 1,250 sorties on their new mount. Except for a *Ramrod* mission on the 2nd, January was very quiet and no operations were flown between the 5th and the 18th as pilots and grounds crews were sent on a gunnery course at Southend. Generally speaking, very bad weather prevented normal air activity during the month anyway. The only thing worth noting is the arrival early in January of the first Mk.VII with a sliding hood. On the operational side, beside scrambles and patrols, the squadron was called upon three times (24th, 25th and 29th) to provide bomber escort. All three operations were uneventful. Activity increased steadily in February mainly because escort to bombers became the rule and not the exception. The squadron participated in a *Ramrod* mission almost every day. It was not, however, during such a mission that 124 opened its score for 1944. On 14 February, two section scrambled, the first at 10.00 (F/O B.P. Brooks and F/Sgt G.J. Beadle – an American serving with the RAF) and the second 35 minutes later (F/Sgt D.P. Kelly and W/O A.E. Nelson - RCAF). They received vectors to the enemy aircraft and the second section soon saw them flying at 16,000 feet. The German aircraft dived inland but Beadle was able to close to within 100 yards of one of them, a Bf109. He opened fire (he was then at 200 feet) and saw strikes on the wing roots before he overshot. Nelson, who was following, fired another long burst at the German aircraft, observed more strikes and eventually saw the

Extracted from wartime footage, Spitfire MD112/ON-F is taxying after a sortie over the Channel in the spring of 1944. Note the small size serial painted on the fuselage band.
(Andrew Thomas)

aircraft crashing into the ground 10 miles south of St-Omer. It was 11.06. In the meantime, Kelly was chasing the other Bf109 and pursued it well over France at zero feet. The hunt lasted for 20 minutesbefore a final burst resulted in the destruction of the '109. The German pilot was, luckily, able to pull up enough high to escape by parachute from his dying aircraft. The day was not over for the squadron, however, as it had the opportunity to engage the enemy once more on a scramble in the afternoon. In the ensuing combat, P/O A.D. Yeardley claimed an Fw190 as damaged. Frustration didn't lasted long for him as eleven days later he had the opportunity to add a confirmed victory to his tally while scrambling to intercept an unidentified aircraft. Yeardley was flying with Sgt G.R. Clarke and the section had taken off at 0920. While at 24,000 feet they sighted vapour trails above and 30 –40 miles ahead travelling south-west. Both pilots dropped their auxiliary tanks and opened up full boost to try to catch the enemy aircraft. They crossed the French coast over Sangatte and wereable to close enough to identify the black crosses and twin engines but not the type. Yeardley got closer and fired a burst and saw the aircraft (a Ju88) diving into ground about 15 miles south of Calais. The rest of the month was eventfulwith close to 250 sorties completed. March was also an active month but operational flying stopped on the 17th. During the first two weeks, the squadron lost one aircraft, the first for five months, when Sgt G.R. G. Clarke was obliged to make a forced landing after the engine caught fire while returning from an uneventful scramble on the 3rd of the month. Fortunately, the pilot escaped injuries. On the 18th, the squadron moved to Church Fenton and at the same time, lost some of its most experienced pilots to other units. P/O Nowell and F/Sgt Kelly were posted to 616 Squadron and F/L 'Ollie' Willis to 501 as a Flight Commander. The rest of the month was spent flying practice flights as far as the weather permitted. The squadron stayed at Church Fenton until 23 April but did not fly any further operations. It returned to 11 Group control when it was sent to Bradwell Bay that day. The pilots were pleased to get closer to an area where something might happen and, on the following day, were back in businesswith two uneventful scrambles to close out the month.

On the first day of May, the squadron participated in Operation 'Fabious', an enormous pre-invasion exercise in the Selsey area. Everybody knew that the invasion of Europe was on the horizon and air activity increased to a record of close to 600 sortiesfor the month, the most sorties since the squadron began flying high altitude Spitfires (VI & VII). However, despite this, and if we exclude a couple of scrambles, the sorties were mainlyboring patrols that were rather frustrating for the pilots. This same level of activity was maintained until D-Day. On this famous day, 6th June, the squadron was airborne early and carried out standing patrols throughout the day. The first was flown by F/L M. Kilburn and F/O J. Melia between 05.20 and 06.50. The squadron wasn't part of the main offensive force and its task was to prevent any reaction from the Luftwaffe over the British Isles. These orders remained unchanged until the 8th when, with a lack of any reaction from the Germans, 124 received permission to carry out a sweep around Brussels. The squadron didn't meet any opposition, but F/L Kilburn, returning from the sweep, was able to shoot up a lorry which blew up. Still continuing its standing patrols, the squadron managed to include the occasional sweep over the continent in its duties. Another was flown on the 11th but proved uneventful. During the patrols, which were now carried out closer to the front, the pilots sometimes had the opportunity to attack targets of opportunity on the ground. On the 12th, control gave some vectors to the section in the air at that time (F/L P. Ayerst and F/LW. 'Jesse' Hibbert, former Malta pilot with 126 Sqn and who will end the war an ace and flying Tempests with 274 Sqn) to intercept an unidentified enemy aircraft and, after a short chase, the pilots were pleased to share a confirmed victory - the 109 crashed into the sea 20 miles east of Dover. Other sweeps were flown on the 13th, 15th, and, on the 17th, the 124 escorted Dakotas which had to land at B.5. This type of escort mission was repeated twice the following day to B.3 and was certainly not without danger as heavy flak was encountered on the last trip. No more sweeps were carried out in June as escort missions took precedence in the second half of the month. June had been a busy month with over 630 sorties completed and more than 1,000 hours flown on the Mk.VIIs. The pilots had already been notified that they would be converting to the HF.IX (High Altitude version) which meant their role would not change for the next few months. In July, the squadron continued to fly mainly patrols, scrambles and escorts while training began on the new HF.IX. By the 21st the squadron had its full complement of HF.IXs but had already flown the first op on type two days earlier. For the Mk.VII, the last mission, a Ramrod sortie - an escort of Lancasters and Halifaxes bombing Caen – was completed on the 18th, and had been led by the CO. The Mk.VII era for the squadron had been rather successful with about ten, mainly reconnaissance, aircraft destroyed – nearly half of the Mk.VII total tally - for the loss of only four aircraft to all causes in 15 months of operations.

Spitfire Mk.VII EN509/ON-G seen in RSU at Odiham circa September 1944. At that time 124 Squadron had already converted to the HF.IX. EN509 was not issued to another squadron after its service with 124. *(CT Collection)*

Claims - 124 Squadron (Confirmed and Probable)

Date	Pilot	SN	Origin	Type	Serial	Code	Nb	Cat.
15.05.43	F/O Oliver E. **Willis**	RAF No. 116663	RAF	Fw190	**BS142**	ON-H	1.0	C
13.06.43	W/O Gareth L. **Nowell** [1]	RAF No. 740499	RAF	Bf109	**MB813**	ON-U	1.0	C
27.06.43	W/O Gareth L. **Nowell** [1]	RAF No. 740099	RAF	Fw190	**MB820**	ON-E	1.0	C
16.08.43	F/O Basil P.K. **Brooks**	RAF No. 124385	RAF	Bf109	**EN505**	ON-S	1.0	C
09.09.43	F/O Paul L. **Philipps**	RAF No. 133837	RAF	Bf109	**MB825**	ON-D	1.0	C
03.10.43	F/Sgt Desmond P. **Kelly**	Aus. 409106	RAAF	Fw190	**EN512**	ON-N	1.0	P
17.10.43	F/Sgt Albert D. **Yeardley**	RAF No. 1430137	RAF	Fw190	**MB826**	ON-J	1.0	C
14.02.44	F/Sgt George J. **Beadle**	RAF No. 1295579	(US)/RAF	Bf109	**EN310**	ON-R	0.5	C
	W/O Albert E. **Nelson**	Can./ R.60066	RCAF		**EN505**	ON-S	0.5	C
	F/Sgt Desmond P. **Kelly**	Aus. 409106	RAAF	Bf109	**MB827**	ON-U	1.0	C
25.02.44	F/O Albert D. **Yeardley**	RAF No. 161082	RAF	Ju88	**MB826**	ON-J	1.0	C
12.06.44	F/L Peter V. **Ayerst**	RAF No. 41362	RAF	Bf109	**MD164**	ON-P	0.5	C
	F/L Walter J. **Hibbert**	RAF No. 120487	RAF		**MD139**	ON-W	0.5	C

Total: 11.0

(1) Actually as a Pilot Officer, officially commisioned on 3 May as 146389 but notification was still to be received

Summary of the aircraft lost on Operations - 124 Squadron

Date	Pilot	S/N	Origin	Serial	Code	Fate
14.05.43	F/Sgt Eric J. **Phelps**	RAF No. 1291762	RAF	**EN496**	ON-U	†
03.03.44	Sgt George R.G. **Clarke**	RAF No. 1317253	RAF	**EN310**	ON-R	-

Total: 2

Summary of the aircraft lost by accident - 124 Squadron

Date	Pilot	S/N	Origin	Serial	Code	Fate
21.05.43	Sgt John H. **Goldworthy**	Aus. 409107	RAAF	**EN457**	ON-C	-
13.10.43	F/Sgt Robert H. **Duckett**	RAF No. 1318397	RAF	**EN512**	ON-N	-

Total: 2

March 1944
October 1944

Victories - confirmed or probable claims: 6.50

First operational sortie: 18.03.44
Last operational sortie: 30.10.44

Number of sorties: ca. 1,880

Total aircraft written-off: 11
Aircraft lost on operations: 9
Aircraft lost in accidents: 2

Squadron code letters:
NX

COMMANDING OFFICERS

S/L James J. O'Meara	RAF No. 40844	RAF	...	29.05.44
S/L Ian N. MacDougall	RAF No. 33491	RAF	29.05.44	14.10.44
S/L Constantine O.J. Pegge	RAF No. 41317	RAF	14.10.44	...

SQUADRON USAGE

When 131 Sqn received its first Mk.VII, the squadron had been flying Spitfires since its formation in June 1941. Mks I, II, V and IX were used during that time. Its CO was S/L James J. O'Meara who was in charge of the squadron for about a year. A very experienced pilot, he had become an ace with No.64 Sqn over Dunkirk and during the Battle of Britain and had served with many more units before taking command of 131. He wore the ribbon of the DFC and Bar on his chest. In March 1944, 131 was based at Colerne (11 Group) and was mainly tasked with carrying out escort missions (*Ramrods*) with its Mk.IXs. However, the Mk.VII was found more suited to this task so a change of Mark was decided at the beginning of 1944.

The first Mk.VIIs were issued at the end of February (MB883, MB935, MD110, MD119, MD120, MD129), followed by one more on 29 February (MD123), one on 2 March (MD160) and two 3 March (MB887, MD134), one on 5 March (MD144) 12 March (MD125) and 20 March (MB932) and, before the month was out, MD168 and MD172 had also arrived. The pilots did not take long to get comfortable with the new mark and the first sorties - an escort mission (*Ramrod*

When 131 Squadron transitioned to the Mk VII, the unit was commanded (from March 1943) by experienced pilot and ace, James 'Orange' O'Meara. A pre-war fighter pilot, he served during the Battles of France and Britain with 64 and 72 Squadrons and 421 Flight and by the end of 1940 he had claimed a dozen of victories and had been awarded the DFC and Bar. He left the unit just before D-Day and was awarded the DSO in October but saw no more operational service until the end of the war. O'Meara chose MD120 'Spirit of Kent' as his personal mount. MD120 was the only presentation Mk VII of the war.

667) for seven Mosquitoes bombing a *Noball* site - was recorded on 18 March. The CO led the mission. However some Mk.IXs were kept until the beginning of April and both types were used simultaneously during a couple of days in March.

In April, the Allies were at the late stage of preparation for the landings in Normandy and all units saw their air activity increased considerably in April and May 1944. After the first few days in April, where low clouds prevailed any operational flying, 131 returned to action on the 6th when two sections scrambled - the first at 15.45 and the second at 20.10,. Both were uneventful. Heavy rain on the 7th and 8th obliged the pilots to rest but on the 9th six Spitfire Mk.VIIs, led by F/L Wooley, were sent to escort a convoy of 24 vessels between Start Point and Portland Bill. Bad weather throughout most of the month but the squadron was able to carry out some *Rodeo* missions on the 12th (but had to return early because of the bad weather), twice on the 17th and 20th but these also proved uneventful. On the 23rd the squadron lost its first pilot and second aircraft since the introduction of the Mk.VII - a Mk.VII had been victim of an accident while taxying on the previous 19th - when, during a scramble, W/O Douglas Philipps lost contact with his wingman, W/O C.J. Crayford, and crashed into the sea 25 miles off Bolt Head. An Australian native of Ireland, Philipps served in various second-line units in the Middle East and UK before joining the squadron in December 1943. The following days were passed on uneventful scrambles and patrols although one Roadstead mission was flown on the 29th but, similiarly, was clear of any trouble.

In May, around 400 sorties were carried out but consisted mainly of patrols and uneventful scrambles. The squadron participated in some *Rodeo*, *Rhubarb* and *Roadstead* missions but otherwise remained more or less in a defensive positionfor the month. A couple of shipping recces were also recorded and it was during such a mission on the 17th that the 131 lost another pilot, F/Sgt Jeffery Morris. Led by F/L Moody (RCAF), four Spitfires had taken off at 05.45 for a shipping reconnaissance when two minesweepers were seen near Lizardrieux and attacked. Believing he had been hit by flak, Morris made an emergency landing 16 km south-west of Lannion but was trapped under his Spitfire and eventually captured by German soldiers. Sent to Paris, he managed to escape, after arriving there on the 18th, when he was taking the Paris Underground. He was hidden in town until 28 August when the city was liberated. The last week of May was marked by two events: a new station for the squadron, Culmhead, was its base from the 24th, and would remain so until the end of August; and a new CO with S/L O'Meara relinquishing command to S/L Ian N. McDougall (a former veteran of the campaign in the Desert in 1942 where he was awarded a DFC with 260 Sqn).

Clifford 'Cliff' Rudland joined the RAF before the war and in June 1940, having completed his training, became a founder member of 263 Squadron as it reformed on Whirlwind twin-engined fighters after the Norwegian debacle. For his second tour he was posted to 131 Squadron as a Flight commander in November 1943 and fought Mk VIIs until he left in August 1944 to take command of 64 Squadron flying Mustangs. Rudland survived the war.
(Chris Goss)

Below:
Spitfire VII MD172 was taken on charge in April 1944 and was flown by various pilots. Its final fate is not totally known as it is stated that it was damaged on operations on 14.06.44 and re-categorised as beyond economic repair later on. However the ORB seems to not be reliable, as MD172 doesn't appear in a Form 541 for that date, so the name of the pilot involved can't be determined.
(Andrew Thomas)

Taken on charge at No.39 MU on 15.02.44, MB935 was issued to No.131 Sqn 11 days later. With high altitude paint scheme, it was flown by various pilots but it was the Irish-born Australian Douglas Phillips who was flying the aircraft when it was lost during a scramble on 23.04.44. Note the codes letters were outlined with black paint which seems to have been discontinued later on. *(Paul Sortehaug)*

On 1 June, led by F/L de Burgh, eight Spitfires took off at 11.40 on *Rhubarb* 265 and flew at sea level to cross the French coast at St Brienne Bay. They remained together until reaching Lamballe then split into two formations of four (one turning west, the other turning east). W/O Atkinson (RAAF) was No.4 in the formation that turned west. They continued, led by F/O Catterall, to fly at ground level. At 12.30, south-west of St-Briec, they saw a goods train of about 15 trucks moving slowly. The attack was ordered but when the flight reformed, Atkinson was not there. It was believed he had been shot down by flak. The squadron returned to patrols and convoy patrols in the following days and, on the 6th, a *Rodeo* mission (165) was carried out with W/C Brothers, the WingCo Flying, flying with the 131. The next day, the squadron was sent off on another *Rhubarb* mission (272) and once more suffered another loss. W/O Woodey, another Australian, was posted missing. During the days following the D-Day landings, the squadron was called to carry out various missions more or less closely connected to the initial actions in Normandy and so the chances of meeting the Luftwaffe increased. That is exactly what happened on the 12th when twelve aircraft took off at 13.00, with 12 Spitfire VIIs of 616 Squadron, for *Rodeo* 169. The Luftwaffe showed up near Le Mans and in the ensuing melee the Fw190s shot down F/L Moody. He was seen going into a steep climb just after crossing the airfield and was heard to say he was going to bale out. 'Junior' Moody was an American-born Canadian of Nova Scotia parents and had served overseas since August 1941. He was first posted to No. 118 Squadron before being posted to Malta the following spring where he served before returning to the UK in October 1942. He had been awarded the DFC while flying with 610 Sqn during his second tour. Moody was not the only loss that day as another Canadian got into some trouble with the Germans and bent the mainplane of his Spitfire due to violent evasive action. The aircraft was later declared as being uneconomical to repair. On the plus side, F/O Parry was able to bag an Fw190. This was the first victory by the squadron with the Mk.VII and the first in almost a year. In the next fortnight 200 more sorties were carried out, mainly *Rodeos*, but *Ramrods* and escort sorties were also flown. No more claims were made during the time but another Spitfire was lost on 21 June. That day, at 17.45, W/O Croydon and F/Sgt Tanner were sent on a shipping recce to St-Peter Port. While approaching from the south, they found 10/10 cloud at 500 feet so, on leaving this layer of cloud, they flew north but ran into accurate and intense flak from the harbour area. Tanner's aircraft was hit but he was able, to continue the journey before the engine cut on approach to Bolt Head and the Spitfire crashed. Luckily, the pilot escaped any injury.

In July and August activity dropped to a bit over 200 sorties per month. Escorts for aircraft operating over Normandy were the most interesting task for the pilots and sometimes they dared to go in at low level to strafe lorries or other ground targets of opportunity like trains. While gratifying for the pilots, this type of mission was not always well suited for the high altitude-rated Mk.VII but many hits were recorded during that period. On 19 August, the Wing, led by W/C Brothers, participated to *Rhubarb* 319 with nine aircraft from 131 Sqn and six more from 616. The latter could not really provide any more aircraft as it had begun its conversion on the Meteor Mk.I. In the area of Mayenne aircraft were reported flying at 2 O'Clock and 10-15 miles away from the formation. The WingCo gave the order to investigate and 131 and 616 found about 30 enemy aircraft flying at 2,000. This formation was lost sight of while the Spitfires were pulling up to drop their 90-gallon tanks. In formation, they started to climb above cloud when Edwards saw and reported aircraft flying below cloud above 10 miles away. The Spitfires dived towards these aircraft and Edwards became separated. He then saw about 16 aircraft at 12 O'Clock and about 2 miles ahead of the formation leader. He reported this and came up behind four aircraft on the right of the low-flying formation. The German aircraft in the far right position broke to starboard and Edwards followed and fired a burst from 250-300 yards but missed. He then turned to the leader of the formation who had turned left after jettisoning his central fuel tank. Edwards followed him and fired again from about 200 yards before a burst from 300 yards hit the aircraft in the tail. He closed on the

Two of the three pilots who made a claim on 7 August 1944 (the last Spitfire Mk VII claims of the war): Peter Brothers, left, was the WingCo Flying of Culmhead wing (131 and 616 Sqns). While flying with 131 he claimed the last of his sixteen confirmed kills on that day which also was the only one he made in a Spitfire Mk VII. He had begun his career before the war and claimed his first victories during the Battle of France while flying Hurricanes. By the end of the Battle of Britain his tally had risen to 12 victories and he had been awarded a DFC. Further postings as CO followed in the next three years and, from January 1943, he led various wings in combat, and received a bar to his DFC and, in November 1944, a DSO. He survived the war and served with the post-war RAF before retiring as an Air Commodore in the 1970s.

Right, 'Sammy' Sampson was another very experienced pilot serving with 131 in early 1944 as a Flight Commander. Even though he left 131 in February for a CGS course, he managed to return to his unit to complete a handful of sorties including the one on 7 August. Later on, he returned to the front line as CO of 127 Sqn before becoming WingCo Flying of 145 Wing of 2 TAF flying Spitfire Mk XVIs. He survived the war with four aircraft destroyed, one probable and a DFC and Bar on his chest.

MD120 was one of the first Mk.VIIs to be allocated to the squadron in February 1944. Another photo of this aircraft exists showing the Horse of Kent painted below the engine cowling (see p14) so we can imagine that it was still painted there when this photo was taken around D-Day but unfortunately the angle of the shot means the wing is hiding the surface the Horse would be on. Note the D-Day markings have been crudely painted on the fuselage and wings. Despite a flying accident on 12.06.44, MD120 continued to serve the squadron until the end of its association with that type. (*Andrew Thomas*)

Bf109 and fired another burst at 150 yards and saw strikes on the cockpit, wing roots and fuselage. The Bf109, pouring glycol, started to catch fire, and Edwards was preparing his final attack when he saw other shots from another Spitfire attacking from below, port and astern. The Bf109 lost its port wing and stalled into the ground. The other pilot Edwards had to share the victory with was P/O Wilson from 616.

By August, 131 was the last operational squadron flying the Mk.VII. No. 611 Squadron – flying the Mk.IX - replaced 616 in the Wing. On 6 August, 131 was sent to the Tours–Chatouroux–Blis area (Rodeo 193). Ground targets were soon found. F/L Waterhouse strafed a staff car and F/Os Parry and Patton damaged a six-wheel lorry. German aircraft were sighted but soon disappeared but eight others were also sighted flying at 2,500 feet. Parry and Patton attacked the formation from a good position and fired at two of them separately. The Fw190 (as they were identified now) shot at by Parry was seen to crash near Argentan while the one hit by Patton was seen abandoned by its pilot after turning towards Le Mans. The next day was also a day to remember. Twelve aircraft led by the WingCo were all airborne by 13.00 for Rodeo 194 (Tours-Blois-Vire area). The formation took off with S/L 'Sammy' Sampson acting as Brothers' wingman. Sampson was a long-service pilot with 131 Sqn up to 1944 before being posted out and eventually serving with HQ 10 Group. It was under the invitation of Brothers that Sampson participated in Rodeo 194. After take-off they headed out across the Channel at zero feet, to avoid German radars, and then climbed when nearing the hostile coast to fly into France, at Cherbourg, at 10,000 feet. Once over the German pocket of resistance there, they descended to 4,000 feet. With about 10 minutes to the return point, they saw two Bf109s flying northwards. At the signal from Pete Brothers, the Spitfires jettisoned their drop tanks and gave chase but the Germans had spotted them early and were too far ahead. Because of this diversion, the Spitfires ended up close to the Château de Blois where they spotted a dozen fighters the British pilots first took to be US Thunderbolts. It didn't take long to realise they were German Fw190s! The Germans manoeuvred to avoid combat and return to their base but Pete Brothers and 'Sammy' Sampson dived after them. The Germans could not escape and soon the British were close enough to open fire and make hits. Brothers attacked the first and it was not long before one the Fw190s was seen to go straight into the ground. It was Brothers' last victory claim. Brothers was not the only one to make a claim as S/L Sampson and F/L 'Closet' Waterhouse (A Flight CO) were also able to shoot down a Fw190 each. Those claims became the last ones for the Mk.VII. The formation returned to base but, en route, Sampson was almost shot down by flak when he took a direct hit from an 88mm anti-aircraft shell which made a large hole in the port wing. Sampson was fortunately able to make a safe landing. The rest of the month was uneventful except on the 25th. At 09.00 that day, eleven aircraft took off from Manston for Culmhead again led by Wing Commander Brothers. Thick cloud was encountered near Salisbury and F/L 'Tete' Bearman, leading Blue section during a climb through cloud, apparently lost control and dived straight into the ground near Old Sarum. There was no chance for the pilot to survive. Three days later the squadron moved to Friston from where they continued their main mission, escort for *Ramrods*. About 200 sorties were carried out in September but no air opposition was encountered as the days of the Mk.VII came to an end at least as far as 131 was concerned. For one of them, however, the end came earlier when on the last day, while returning from an escort of 36 Marauders, the engine of the aircraft flown by F/O Baxter lost oil pressure. The pilot was obliged to make a force landing between Ghand and Brussels in Belgium. The aircraft broke its back during the process but Baxter escaped major injury. He was admitted to RAF Hospital Wroughton on 6 October 1944 suffering from concussion and contusion of the knee. He had joined the squadron in June and upon recovery was posted to No. 453 (RAAF) Sqn in April 1945. He left for repatriation in November and served in the RAAF post-war. In October only 110 sorties could be flown as bad weather prevented much operational flying although about a dozen of *Ramrod* missions were be carried out. The last of them, on the 30th, (*Ramrod* 1353 – Lancasters bombing Welcheren) saw the aircraft returning after 2 hours and 10 minutes of flight and nothing to report. The following day the squadron was stood down to prepare for deployment to the Far East, under the new CO since mid-October, S/L Pegge, a Battle of Britain veteran. The Mk.VIIs were handed over to the newly reformed 154 Squadron.

No.131 Squadron became somewhat unique when it converted to the Spitfire Mk VII in Spring 1944. The Mk VII was the first major re-design of the Spitfire and was dedicated to high altitude flying operations. Only 141 were built, hence only several units became operational on the type, including No. 131 (the third unit to have been transitioned). From June 1943 the PRU Blue camouflage and markings were the norm for the Mk VII but from Spring 1944, as the Mk VII was no more used as a high altitude fighter, some Mk VIIs began to be repainted with the standard Day Fighter Scheme and had new rounded wing tips installed (like MD183 seen here which was issued to 131 on 19 June 1944). It is rather rare to get to see both sides of an aircraft and the two shots show the elegant silhouette of the Spitfire Mk VII. It is seen flying at the end of July 1944 when the D-Day stripes had been partially deleted.

Taken from various angles and time, Spitfire MD111 served with No.131 Sqn between February and October 1944. The two photos below show it somewhere at the end of July 1944 while the photo above was probably later in the summer with various dirty marks around the engine and on the fuselage. The spinner seems to have been painted white by that time. Note in the background, a camouflaged Mk.VII coded NX-S.

Claims - 131 Squadron (Confirmed and Probable)

Date	Pilot	SN	Origin	Type	Serial	Code	Nb	Cat.
12.06.44	F/O Robert K. **Parry**	RAF No. 156705	RAF	Bf109	**MD187**	NX-V	1.0	C
06.08.44	F/O Robert K. **Parry**	RAF No. 156705	RAF	Fw190	**MD134**	NX-P	1.0	C
	W/O Harold A. **Patton**	Aus. 414262	RAAF	Fw190	**MD173**		1.0	C
19.07.44	F/O Geoffrey A.B. **Edwards**	RAF No. 142070	RAF	Fw190	**MD143**		0.5	C
07.08.44	W/C Peter M. **Brothers**	RAF No. 37668	RAF	Fw190	**MD188**	PB	1.0	C
	S/L Ralph W.L. **Sampson**	RAF No. 116753	RAF	Fw190	**MD165**	NX-M	1.0	C
	F/L John C.R. **Waterhouse**	RAF No. 112749	RAF	Fw190	**MD152**		1.0	C

Total: 6.50

Summary of the aircraft lost on Operations - 131 Squadron

Date	Pilot	S/N	Origin	Serial	Code	Fate
23.04.44	W/O Douglas F. **Philipps**	Aus. 401394	RAAF	**MB935**	NX-Z	†
17.05.44	F/Sgt Jeffrey E. **Morris**	RAF No. 1390161	RAF	**MD166**		-
01.06.44	W/O Wiliam J. **Atkinson**	Aus. 413332	RAAF	**MB887**		†
07.06.44	W/O Jack E. **Woodey**	Aus. 411625	RAAF	**MB883**		†
12.06.44	F/L Vincent K. **Moody**	Can./ J.15362	RCAF	**MD123**		†
	W/O James S. **Hannah**	Can./ R.99388	RCAF	**MD128**		-
14.06.44	*No details available*			**MD172**	NX-L	-
21.06.44	F/Sgt Ernest J. **Tanner**	RAF No. 1323017	RAF	**MD131**		-
30.09.44	F/O John R. **Baxter**	Aus. 419922	RAAF	**MD119**		Inj.

Total: 9

Summary of the aircraft lost by accident - 131 Squadron

Date	Pilot	S/N	Origin	Serial	Code	Fate
19.04.44	F/L Vincent K. **Moody**	Can./ J.15362	RCAF	**MB932**		-
25.08.44	F/L Cecil E. **Bearman**	RAF No. 122343	RAF	**MD171**		†

Total: 2

September 1943
December 1944

Victories - confirmed or probable claims: 4.50

First operational sortie: 11.09.43
Last operational sortie: 31.07.44

Number of sorties: ca. 1,520
Total aircraft written-off: 12
Aircraft lost on operations: 9
Aircraft lost in accidents: 3

Squadron code letters:
YQ

COMMANDING OFFICERS

S/L Leslie W. Watts	RAF No. 117728	RAF	...	23.07.44
W/C Andrew McDowall	RAF No. 89299	RAF	23.07.44	...

SQUADRON USAGE

As with 124 Squadron, 616 was operating the Mk.VI when it began to convert to the Mk.VII. When the first Mk.VIIs arrived at the Squadron in September 1943, the unit, stationed at Ibley, was commanded by S/L Leslie Watts who had taken command in July 1943 and, in the same month, been awarded the DFC for his excellent service with the 616. No transition was needed and the Mk.VIIs were introduced into the Squadron's inventory without problems. Even operational flights were carried out with both marks during this time. The first sorties were recorded on the 11th when F/L Danville and F/Sgt Woodacre took off at 1910 for an uneventful scramble before being recalled soon after crossing the English Coast. Two days later, a mixed section of one Mk.VI and one Mk.VII took off to investigate a plot of three aircraft flying over Cherbourg. They patrolled at 22,000 feet in the neighbourhood of Alderney. Flight Sergeant Dean, who was flying the Mk.VII, indeed saw three aircraft over Cherbourg, at four miles range, but could not get closer to make an attack. The Mk.VII was involved in seven more scrambles for the rest of the month and all were uneventful. The introduction of the mark was slow as by the end of the month only five Mk.VIIs were on squadron charge.

In October, the Mk.VIIs continued with regular scrambles while the Mk.VIs were now reserved for convoy patrol duty. On the 9th the Mk.VII was used for the time on an escort mission. S/L Watts led three other Mk.VIIs to provide high escort to 24 Mitchells which were to bomb the airfield of Brest-Guipavas. The four aircraft operated at 28,000 feet and returned after 1 hour and 30 minutes without any incident to report. On the 13th a new B Flight CO arrived at the squadron, F/L Michael Graves, posted from 610 Sqn. He had been awarded the DFC while fighting over Malta in 1942 and had claimed four confirmed victories and four more probables flying there with 126 squadron. His first operational flight in the Mk.VII was a scramble two days after his arrival. That day, S/L Watts led a shipping recce but returned with nothing of interest to report. With more Mk.VIIs arriving, the mark was progressively flying more and more sorties. The Mk.VII had still not totally supplanted the Mk.VI in November as, during the month, little operational flying was done (only 40 sorties). Despite this, 616 lost its first Mk.VII and, unfortunately, its first pilot too when, on the 5th, while returning from a convoy patrol, Sgt Gordon's engine failed about five miles off Portland. He was seen landing on the sea. Immediately, boats were sent from the convoy to try to rescue the pilot but no trace of him was ever found despite an ASR section from the squadron combing the area. Bad luck continued for 616 when another aircraft and pilot were lost on 3 December. That day, in the middle of the afternoon, four aircraft were dispatched to provide an escort to a VIP aircraft but the Spitfires had to return due to deteriorating weather. F/Sgt Rutherford crashed his aircraft while making his landing approach at Exeter and died a couple of hours later of his injuries. On the positive side, 616 was now fully operational on the Mk.VII, keeping a handful of Mk.VIs for training purposes, but the poor weather of December 1943 curtailed operational sorties with less than 70 mainly scrambles and convoy patrols being carried out for the month. However, 616 was also called on fly 'exciting' missions like escort to Typhoons (as on the 24th and 31st). For the latter, the squadron flew, for the first time, 12 Mk.VIIs over Morlaix and St- Briene. Half of the formation made a U-turn upon reaching the French coast while the remaining six aircraft swept the target without incident.

January was quiet with less than 100 sorties flown. Only a few operations towards the Cherbourg area were recorded beside the routine weather reconnaissance flights. Two fighter sweeps were flown on the 4th and 5th, involving eight aircraft each, with an ope-

By summer 1944, 616 Sqn was led by experienced pilots. Left, a former Malta veteran, Les Watts fought with Nos.603 and 249 Sqns during the worst months of the Malta siege in 1942 and was able to make several claims. For his second tour he was posted to 616 Sqn in June 1943, then 322 (Dutch) Sqn, both as a Flight Commander before returning to the squadron as CO. He remained with 616 until his death on 29.04.45 while flying a Meteor.
Right, Dennis Barry joined 616 early 1944 from 504 Sqn. Like Watts, he later transitioned onto the Meteor. He survived the war.

rational ceiling of 22,000 feet. The only other operation of interest that month was a sweep - *Ramrod* - over Cambrai. Departing Kenley, thirteen aircraft took off at 15.20 in the hope of intercepting some Luftwaffe aircraft. However, at this stage of the war, the Luftwaffe had seen its combat priorities change to intercepting American 'heavies' and no German fighters were encountered. Sadly, that didn't prevent the loss of F/O A.K. Dolton who had reported, on the return trip, that he had fuel problems and would be unable to reach England. He then chose to return over the continent to bail out but, before he was able to take to his parachute, Fw190s from JG26 attacked and shot him down. Dolton still managed to bail out but sooner than he had planned! He spent the rest of the war in a POW camp. February 1944 can be seen as the first month of real operational activity since the conversion to the Mk.VII although only 119 sorties were flown. These consisted of offensive sweeps, scrambles and escort missions alongside boring convoy patrols but the pilots had the feeling that their daily job was becoming more interesting. Some of those missions were flown from Ford near Chichester (closer to the Continent) but Tangmere and Martlesham Heath were also setting-off points. Despite this new activity, no contact with the enemy was reported nor was there any loss of any kind.

The first fortnight of March was similar to February but in the middle of the month the squadron left Exeter for West Malling where operations continued as normal. Before the month ended, the 616 received new pilots to replace those posted out. Two arrived from 124 Sqn with experience on the Mk.VII. Flying Officer G.L. Nowell, a very experienced pilot with DFM & Bar and 16 claims to his credit (including two on the Mk.VII), arrived to take a Flight Commander post. With him came F/Sgt Kelly, an Australian, with one confirmed and one damaged enemy aircraft to his credit. These experienced pilots really boosted the potential of the squadron. March was a quiet month (about 170 sorties) with few offensive operations and uneventful convoy patrols and several scrambles proving the norm. After months of uneventful missions, and no claims reported in over six months (and the last claim was while flying the Mk.VI), something at last happened in April 1944. However, the month started badly for the squadron. The weather was poor on the first day of the month when two aircraft were scrambled at 13.25. The section was composed of F/O Clegg and an Australian pilot, Flight Sergeant D.E. Johnston. They were vectored to the Isle of Wight. Soon after take-off the section was lost in cloud and F/O Clegg returned to base alone at 14.05. Johnston was posted missing but was soon found dead in the wreckage of his Spitfire, having crashed near Tangmere. For the ensuing days, convoy patrols followed uneventful scrambles and uneventful scrambles followed convoy patrols with nothing to report each time. But, on the 21st, luck was on 616's side. At 11.40, F/O A.G.P. Jennings and P/O Jean Clerc (a recently commissioned Free French pilot) were scrambled and vectored to the Cherbourg peninsula and arrived near Maupertus airfield before orbiting at 13,000 feet as enemy aircraft had been reported in the area. Jennings decided to go down to investigate and soon saw an Fw190 landing at Maupertus. Clerc broke away and came down astern of the now taxiing aircraft on the airfield. Closing to 300 yards, Clerc fired at the Fw190 which was seen to explode in flames and smoke. Jennings followed Clerc and fired at the burning Fw190 which was therefore completely destroyed. Both pilots left the area at once and on the way back over Cherbourg they were caught by flak, which damaged Clerc's aircraft, but both were able to land safely back at base after close to two hours of flight. Flak almost claimed a squadron Spitfire the next day when W/O D.P. Kelly's aircraft was hit. Kelly was wounded in the left eye by shrapnel during an Isle of Wight patrol that had been vectored over Cherbourg. Almost blinded, Kelly called up his leader, F/O Nowell, who came alongside and helped him to return to base by guiding him down to a safe landing. Kelly's wounds would keep him away from the squadron for many weeks. The month ended with an escort of FAA Avengers heading for ashipping strike off Ushant. The enemy vessels were not found and the mission was uneventful and the formation returned to base after 2 hours and 20 minutes of flight. During the month close to 250 sorties were carried out.

May was a busy month with 400 sorties completed. With the invasion of Europe looming, patrols over the Channel were the bulk of the daily duty and, as usual, were uneventful. The first offensive op of the month was flown on the 22nd when the A Flight CO, Dennis Barry, led four aircraft on a *Rhubarb* mission to shoot up any trains or military targets in the Avranches-Rennes-Lamballe area. While attacking trains in Folligny yards, F/S Prouting's aircraft was hit by flak from an armoured train and was seen to crash in flames just outside the village. He was the first pilot of 616 to be killed by enemy action since the conversion to the Mk.VII the previous September. The next day, F/L Graves led 12 Spitfires on an escort mission – *Ramrod* 131 - of RAF Mitchells which had to bomb Dinard airfield.

Jack McG. Cleland was a New Zealander and one of the four pilots to make a claim in the Spitfire VII while the type was on strength with 616 Sqn (and the only double claims ever on this mark). He had been posted to the squadron in November 1944 for his second tour. He left a couple of weeks later just before the transition onto the Meteor. His next assignment was no less interesting, however, as he was posted to the USAAF's 363rd FS, 357th FG, flying Mustangs and based at Leiston (Suffolk). He consequently became the only Kiwi fighter pilot to fly with the Eighth Air Force. He returned to 616 after two months of operations. *(T.R. Allonby via Paul Sortehaug)*

Above, Cleland returned, on 23 September 1944, to visit his American colleagues in a Spitfire Mk VII - MD182, one of the last Spitfires still on squadron charge. The aircraft is seen here with an American pilot sitting in the cockpit - Norbert Fisher - and another on the cowling - William Fricker.
(Paul Sortehaug)

Only one more offensive mission was reported before the month ended, on the 28th, during which two more trains were attacked. All aircraft returned to base safely. For the month, the tally was quite impressive with eight locomotives attacked, as well as six railway wagons, one staff car, two lorries, one RDF station and one gun post. Training was carried out alongside these missions and, on one such exercise, the squadron lost one Spitfire Mk.VII in an accident on the 12th. Returning from an air to air firing exercise, the pilot, the French P/O Clerc, found himself landing short and to avoid hitting the ground, decided to raise the undercarriage. He decided to land, instead of going around for another approach, but eventually overshot with the undercarriage still retracted. The aircraft was later declared damaged beyond economical repair. June started in the evening with a *Rhubarb* mission during which two more locomotives and six wagons were added to the squadron's score. All the aircraft returned safely to base although the Spitfire flown by F/L Barry, who was leading the attack, was damaged by flak. In the next days, only patrols or convoy patrols were carried out. In all 111 sorties were flown in the first five days of June with 48 flown on the 5th alone.

On D-Day, 616 started operations after mid-day, as they were not part of the first forces to provide support for the landing troops. Also, as the sky was rather full of aircraft, the pilots did not fly that morning. In the afternoon only patrols were flown and in the evening the CO, S/L Watts, took off at 20.30 to lead a sweep over the Brest peninsula. The pilots returned to base at 22.50 with nothing to report. The next day, eight aircraft took off at 05.25 to attack transport targets inland of the beachhead and when the Spitfires returned to base they could claim the damage of two locomotives and one truck. Flak was not absent and succeeded in damaging F/L G.N. Honson's aircraft. Late in the afternoon, the CO led another attack during which two more locomotives and two lorries were added to the squadron's score. On 9 June, the squadron flew its first 'Beachhead patrol' to help ensure the Luftwaffe did not interfere with the landings as the beachhead was now developing and expanding. Other ground targets were attacked the next day and hits were recorded on one locomotive and trucks but the engine of F/L Graves' aircraft gave signs of trouble and he was forced to ditch 40 miles south of Start Point. Graves was eventually rescued by a Walrus. It is worth noting that F/L Cleland had already jettisoned his hood and was prepared to throw out his dinghy when he saw Graves climbing into his own dinghy. Operational flying continued as usual until the 12th which was a day to remember. The day started like any other but, in the afternoon, Culmhead Wing took off led by its WingCo Flying, W/C Brothers, and in company with 131 Sqn. The object of the mission - *Rodeo* 169 - was to shoot up enemy aircraft reported to have moved to the airfields at Le Mans and Laval. The squadron acted as top cover while the Spitfires of 131 Sqn attacked Le Mans. The role was reversed over Laval airfield with 131 staying at 5,000 feet. At that moment, F/L G.A. Harrison and F/O J.K. Rodger attacked a Bf109 and the latter opened fire while Harrison broke away to fly towards another enemy aircraft. Rodger saw the wing tip of Harrison's Spitfire tear off the tail of the enemy before flying on. The German pilot bailed out his aircraft which dove into the ground and exploded. A few seconds later Harrison's propeller was seen to stop and he was heard to say that he was preparing to bail out when his aircraft dived into the ground from 1,000 feet. Other victories were claimed - one Bf109 by the Australian W/O Hart and two Fw190s by the New Zealander F/L Jack Cleland. Other pilots strafed the airfield and damaged other German fighters in the process (two were left burning). However it was not over yet for the pilots of 616 as Cleland was soon hit by flak. Escorted by his squadron mates, he headed to base but the engine finally failed upon reaching the English Coast and he had no choice but to bail out. He was picked up by an ASR launch right away and was back with the squadron before the day was out. Despite the loss of two aircraft and one pilot, 12 June was the first real success for 616 for many months. Normal duties continued to be carried out over the following days and, while no more claims were made for the rest of June, the squadron reported a sad loss. On the 19th, while carrying out a shipping recce in the Gulf of St-Malo, and off the Cherbourg Peninsula, W/O R.A. Hart (RAAF) had his engine cut out. He tried to gain height to bail out but the aircraft stalled and crashed before he had time to do so. His body was never recovered. On the 22nd, with the Wing, 616 provided escort to 20 Lancasters which had to bomb the V-1 storage site at Wizernes. The operation was repeated two days later, with a mixed force of Lancasters and Halifaxes this time, and the target was located in the northern part of France in the Pas de Calais. Poor weather in the last days of June prevented much flying. Despite this, the squadron had to report the death of Sgt Vic Allen who had taken off heading for Herefordshire where his parents lived. Flying over their village, he began to pull up into a barrel roll but failed to recover and dived into the ground while his horrified parents watched. In June 616 completed close to 375 sorties, its best record as far as the Mk.VII is concerned.

July would be the last month of flying the Mk.VII. Indeed the 616 had been already been chosen to become the first jet fighter unit of the RAF with the Meteor. Already, in June, some pilots had been sent to Farnborough to be introduced to the new British jet fighter. In the meantime, sorties had to be continued with the now ageing Mk.VII. Rangers, shipping recces and fighter sweeps were the main tasks the squadron had to fly during the month. All of these missions were uneventful except on the 11th when F/O Cooper (from Kenya) was hit in his right foot by flak but managed to return home safely before being hospitalised. The next day the two first Meteors arrived at the squadron marking the beginning of the end for the Spitfire Mk.VII with 616. However, the Mk.VII would leave on a high when, on the 19th, during one of the last Mk.VII ops, 616 provided several aircraft for *Rhubarb* 319. Wing Commander Brothers again led 616 and 131. Enemy fighters were encountered near Mayenne and Ian Wilson was able to share in the destruction of a Bf109 having seen strikes in the wing roots, cockpit and fuel tanks after firing from 200 yards, closing in dead astern, and breaking off at 100 yards. He

Some Belgians flew with 616 while it was equipped with the Mk.VII. Left, Marcel Mullenders was a former pre-war Belgian military pilot and took part in the combats of May-June 1940. He succeeded in escaping from Belgium at the end of 1941 and enlisted in the RAF upon his arrival in England. Posted to 616 at the end of his training, he remained with the squadron until early February 1945 and became one of the first Belgians to have flown the Meteor in operations in the meantime. He survived the war and served with the post-war Belgian Air Force, becoming the first CO of the first jet fighter unit of the Belgian Air Force - 350 Sqn. Jean Ost - right - was a young Belgian who enlisted in the RAF in August 1941 and had completed his training by mid-1943. He was posted to 616 on 24 March 1944 from No.186 Sqn and, with Mullenders, was one of only two Belgians on the squadron by Spring 1944. He seems to have left before D-Day. *(André Bar)*

then saw the '109 crashing into woods near Alençon (see 131 Sqn part for more details). The Meteors began to be engaged in anti-diver patrols on the 27th as one flight was now operational on the jet while the Spitfires of the other flight (B) continued to fly weather recces only. The last sortie was reported on the 31st with F/L Clegg and F/S Easy marking the end of the operations on the Mk.VII with 616. However it seems that did not put an end to the association with 616 totally as a handful of aircraft was kept on charge for training and hack work. Indeed the Meteor was a rare bird and, to keep the pilots flying current, it was thought prudent to keep some Mk.VIIs on charge for non-operational tasks. It was during one such training flight, on 5 December, that F/Sgt Watts ran off the runway, after landing at Brockworth, and tipped up on his nose. No further record of any use of the Mk.VII is noted after this date but it is likely 616

Claims - 616 Squadron (Confirmed and Probable)

Date	Pilot	SN	Origin	Type	Serial	Code	Nb	Cat.
12.06.44	W/O Robert A. **Hart**	Aus. 408257	RAAF	Bf109	**MB808**	YQ-F	1.0	C
	F/L Geoffrey A. **Harrison**	RAF No.60102	RAF	Bf109	**MD121**		1.0	C
	F/L Jack McG. **Cleland**	NZ411371	RNZAF	Fw190	**MB768**	YQ-X	2.0	C
19.07.44	P/O Ian T. **Wilson**	RAF No. 177659	RAF	Fw190	**MD108**	YQ-E	0.5	C

Total: 4.50

Summary of the aircraft lost on Operations - 616 Squadron

Date	Pilot	S/N	Origin	Serial	Code	Fate
05.11.43	Sgt Walter **Gordon**	RAF No. 1016772	RAF	**MB929**	YQ-J	†
03.12.43	F/Sgt Frank W. **Rutherford**	RAF No. 1497152	RAF	**MB930**	YQ-R	†
21.01.44	F/O Alfred K. **Doulton**	RAF No.143226	RAF	**MB913**	YQ-G	PoW
01.04.44	F/Sgt Donald E. **Johnston**	Aus. 412550	RAAF	**MD116**	YQ-K	†
22.05.44	P/O George E. **Prouting**	RAF No. 175505	RAF	**MD108**	YQ-E	†
10.06.44	F/L Michael A. **Graves**	RAF No. 69475	RAF	**MD104**	YQ-R	-
12.06.44	F/L Geoffrey A. **Harrison**	RAF No .60102	RAF	**MD121**		†
	F/L Jack McG. **Cleland**	NZ411371	RNZAF	**MB768**	YQ-X	-
19.06.44	W/O Robert A. **Hart**	Aus. 408257	RAAF	**MD133**	YQ-N	†

Total: 9

Summary of the aircraft lost by accident - 616 Squadron

Date	Pilot	S/N	Origin	Serial	Code	Fate
12.05.44	P/O Jean **Clerc**	F.30795	FFAF	**MD106**	YQ-W	-
29.06.44	Sgt Victor J.T. **Allen**	RAF No. 1579427	RAF	**MB762**		†
05.12.44	F/Sgt Philip G. **Watts**	RAF No. 1177637	RAF	**MD137**		-

Total: 3

With Other Fighter Units

Actually, there is one more squadron that used the Mk.VII as its main equipment on operations: 154 Sqn. This Spitfire unit had flown for two years in North Africa and over Italy and the south of France when it was disbanded on 29 October 1944. The squadron was reformed on 16 November at Biggin Hill and took over No.131 Squadron's 21 Spitfire Mk.VIIs as the latter had been withdrawn from ops pending a move overseas. The CO chosen to lead 154 was Squadron Leader Gerald J. Stonhill and new pilots soon became to arrive at the squadron. Most were beginning their second tour. All, except for one Australian pilot, were British. Owing to bad weather, training on a regular basis became difficult but when 154 became officially operational, on 14 January, about 350 hours had been logged. Bomber escort was the main task given to the squadron. The same day, 154 recorded its first loss when F/O Hurst crashed 1.5 miles NW of Biggin Hill during a training flight for unknown reasons. He was buried in his home town of Rochester the following day. Bad luck continued during January as, 11 days later, a Canadian Dakota crashed on take-off at Biggin Hill destroying one the squadron's Spitfires in the process but fortunately without more serious consequences for 154.

Operations began on the first day of February with an uneventful escort of Lancasters to Munchen led by the CO. In the next fortnight, the squadron was airborne on six days but except for one op over enemy territory all escorts were carried out over Allied controlled areas. The last escort mission, an escort of captured Bf109s, was carried out on the 14th and was flown by Flying Officers Knowles and Fleming and Flight Sergeants D. Bourne and G. Pritchard (the last four of 41 operational sorties recorded in all by 154). This flight marked an end to the operational career of the Mk.VII as, earlier in the month, the first Mustang Mk. IVs had begun to arrive at the squadron. The Spitfires left progressively for storage and by the end of the month none were on charge.

Philip N.G. Knowles (left) was one of the pilots posted to 154 Sqn in February 1945. It was his second tour and he flew twice on operations including the last operational sortie on the 14.02.45. When 154 was disbanded he was posted to 126 Sqn, flying Mustangs, and ended the war with this unit.
Spitfire Mk.VII MD111/HG-Q, seen at Biggin Hill in February 1945. Just behind, an uncoded Mustang Mk.IV, one of the first received by the squadron.

Summary of the aircraft lost by accident - 154 Squadron

Date	Pilot	S/N	Origin	Serial	Code	Fate
14.01.45	F/O Albert H. Hurst	RAF No. 150381	RAF	MD165		†
25.01.45	-	-	-	MD134		-

Total: 2

MD168 was one of the 21 Spitfire Mk.VIIs inherited from 131 Sqn on 23.11.44. It is seen with F/O William N. Fleming on board during a training flight. Fleming was also posted to 126 Sqn when 154 was disbanded. It is believed that 154 kept the individual letters in use with 131.

Known as «Ian», John Blair was a former Observer who had flown on Blenheims in the Middle East with No.113 Sqn in 1940. He was awarded the DFM when he managed to fly the Blenheim back after its pilot had been killed by enemy action. He retrained as a pilot and was posted to No.501 Sqn. On 25.04.42 his Spitfire was damaged by flak and force-landed near Worth Maltravers, Dorset. Hospitalised and returned to operations one year later, he was posted to No.602 Sqn in March 1943. He was commissioned in October 1943 and completed his tour in May 1944. *(Many Souffan)*

Contrary to its forerunner, the Mk.VI, the Mk.VII wasn't used by many other fighter units. The Mk.VI was used in small numbers by about half a dozen fighter units generally based in the far north where the chance of enemy encounters was minimal (and usually alongside old Mk.V units). This wasn't the case for the Mk.VII. No unit as such received any Mk.VIIs but some fighter units sent north to rest - Orkney Islands and its base, Skeabrae -, had the opportunity to use the Mk.VII allocated to the Station Flight. Usually, one flight of the squadrons sent north was based at Skeabrae on detachment while the other flight remained at Sumburgh using old Mk.Vs. Over a year the following squadrons turned over at the Orkneys: 312 (Czech), 118, 453 (RAAF), 602 and 313 (Czech). Little activity was noticed and the opportunity to fly a Mk.VII was seen as being the most attractive to do. As far as the Mk.VII was concerned, while at the Station Flight Skeabrae at the end of summer 1943, 312 didn't report any operational flights with the Mk.VII between August and October. No.118 Squadron, which followed in October, also had no use for the Mk.VII and 453 only flew one uneventful scramble 7 November (F/O McDermott in MB828/Y and P/O Ferguson in MB765/G) to 37,000 feet without results, the three apparent bandits vanishing. Only three flights out of 50 were carried out on the Mk.VII in November and two of 50 in December with none at all in January. No. 453 Squadron was replaced by 602 in mid-January 1944 but the Mk.VII was only used to complement aircraft numbers and was not regarded as main equipment. Three flights (of 14) were recorded in January and four out of 50 in February but, while the number was small, 602 would have the chance to claim the first of the two victories by a Mk.VII in the area. Indeed, on 20 February, F/L W.G. Bennetts and F/O 'Ian' Blair had already made an uneventful scramble at 10.55 in Mk.Vs when they were called for another scramble two hours later, Bennetts taking off this time in Mk.VII MB763 and Blair in MD114 (Blair leading the section). They climbed to 32,000 feet very quickly and soon vapour trails were sighted. At the same moment ground control confirmed that it was an enemy aircraft. Blair pushed the throttle forward and the speed increased in an attempt to reach the German. However the German saw the Spitfires and he turned for home. Both British pilots followed him and Blair opened fire at extreme range without results. Bennett soon opened fire too but at a distance of 250 yards. Unfortunately, his gun sight packed up and he had to break off. Blair then closed and fired a burst from 200 yards. The burst was accurate as the starboard wing of the German aircraft broke off and fell into the sea. The pilot, *Oberleutnant* Helmut Quednau of 1.(F)/120 was killed in his Bf109 G-6/R3 coded A6+XH. Debris from the German aircraft hit the radiator of Blair's aircraft and he made a forced landing at Stronsay without major consequences for pilot or machine. No. 602 Squadron was replaced by 118 and then by the Czech 313. No. 118 recorded only two scrambles during the stay in Scotland. - on 21 May (W/O A. Taylor in MD122 and F/Sgt C.H.P. Baytun in MD138) and 30 May (F/O J.J. Parker RAAF in MD118 and W/O A. Taylor in MD138). The first section returned to base with nothing to report but the second section shot down a Ju88 about 25 miles east of Kirkall. It was the second and last victory recorded by a Spitfire Mk.VII based in the Orkneys. No. 313 Squadron, which arrived on 11 July, was different to the two other Czech fighter squadrons in that a significant number of its pilots were non-Czech. The squadron was commanded by Alois Hochmal, a pre-war Czechoslovakian military pilot. Operations began the following day and uneventful scrambles patrols were recorded that month but, generally speaking, air activity was low as with the previous squadrons. In the meantime pilots of 313 continued to use their time to fly the aircraft of the Skeabrae Station Flight (usually to train 313 pilots with no experience on type). It was during one such flight, that a British pilot of 313 wrecked Mk.VII MB763 when he overshot the landing and tipped up (15 July). The Mk.VII seems to have been used in July and August only. This kind of loan seems to have stopped in August. Perhaps the loss of MB763 was the cause for this change!

Claims - 602 Squadron (Confirmed and Probable)

Date	Pilot	SN	Origin	Type	Serial	Code	Nb	Cat.
20.02.44	P/O John **Blair**	RAF No. 53630	RAF	Bf109	**MD114**	DU-G	1.0	C
					Total: 1			

Claims - 118 Squadron (Confirmed and Probable)

Date	Pilot	SN	Origin	Type	Serial	Code	Nb	Cat.
30.05.44	P/O John J. **Parker**	Aus. 412829	RAAF	Ju88	**MD118**		0.5	C
	W/O Alfred **Taylor**	RAF No. 1019604	RAF		**MD138**		0.5	C
			Total: 1					

In summer 1944, 313 (Czech) was sent for a rest in the Orkneys. The squadron was commanded at that time by Alois Hochmal, a pre-war Czechoslovakian military pilot who had escaped to France before the war. He enlisted in the French Air Force then fled to the UK when France collapsed. He briefly served with Nos.247 and 501 Sqns before arriving at 313 Sqn in May 1941. In May 1944, while undertaking his second tour, he was given command of 313 and remained in this role until September. After the war he joined the new Czechoslovakian Air Force. *(Jiri Rajlich)*

Below, even wearing the codes 'DU' of 312 (Czech) Sqn, Spitfire HF.VII MD114 belonged to Station Flight Skaebrae in February 1944. It was never used by 312 but the codes were added when the squadron was based there. When it left in September 1943, the codes were kept and the squadrons which replaced 312 continued to fly the Mk.VIIs with the same codes. Indeed it was customary for aircraft, whether Mk.V, Mk.VI or Mk.VII, to remain at Skaebrae (allowing for normal rotation of overhauls) and units posted normally consisted of pilots and ground crew who left their original aircraft behind and took over the ones based at Skaebrae. There was a shortage of Spitfire Mk.IXs, which were needed for the 2nd TAF, whereas Orkney was seen to be adequately defended by Mk Vs and a handful of high altitude marks. While stationed at Skaebrae the Czechs used three Spitfire.VIIs (MB763/DU-W, MB765 and MB828).

Whatever the reason the high-altitude Spitfires retained their DU codes and later there was another Spitfire VII, MD122, coded DU-Z.

It is believed this situation came about as an oversight by the squadron which replaced 312 and then became an entrenched practice. This is probably one of the few cases, if not the only one, when two UK-based RAF fighter units used the same code at the same time. Below, MD114/DU-G in which P/O made his claim in February 1944. *(J. Blair via Peter Arnold)*

Summary of the aircraft lost by accident - 313 Squadron

Date	Pilot	S/N	Origin	Serial	Code	Fate
15.07.44	P/O Robert E. **Dodds**	RAF No. 172864	RAF	**MB763**	DU-Z	-
		Total: 1				

Another Spitfire of SF Skeabrae - above and below right – Mk.VII DU-Z (MD122), and below the results of the accident of MB763/DU-W flown by a 313 Squadron pilot. The Mk VII based at Skaebrae were officially allocated to the Station Flight of the base. The fighter units were regularly turned over at Skeabrae, and their pilots frequently used the Mk VIIs generally for type experience and the occasional operational sortie. *(Jiri Rajlich)*

WITH OTHER UNITS

The Spitfire Mk.VII, as with the Mk.VI, was also found to be useful for the RAF's meteorological reconnaissance units. As there were enough Mk.VIs, the need for the Mk.VII was limited and only about 10 were used by the Met units, 1402 Flight and Nos. 518 and 519 Squadrons. Furthermore, they weren't used until Autumn 1944 when the Mk.VI began to be phased out. The Mk.VII was used to carry out PRATA flights (PRessure And Temperature Ascent). All their armament was removed (as with the Mk.VI). If we take, for example, 519 Squadron, over 300 such flights were flown up to VE-Day with a further 375 by December 1945 when the type was withdrawn from use. These flights were normally flown twice a day. Two accidents were recorded in 519's records. The first occurred on 10 June 1945 when the Spitfire flown by F/L J.C. Steele suffered an engine failure at high altitude. It was caused by an engine over-speed and all temperatures quickly began to reach their maximum. Fortunately, the pilot managed to reach the base at Wick where he made a successful belly-landing. The second loss occurred five months later during a training flight. While flying in cloud, the pilot, F/Sgt W.A. Sperry lost control due to the failure of the artificial horizon. The pilot regained control of the aircraft and landed at Leuchars. At first sight the aircraft was not damaged but, after investigation, it was discovered that the wings had been over-stressed during the recovery process. The Spitfire was then declared un-repairable.

From Spring 1945 onwards, the Spitfire Mk.VII began to be issued to some Air Gunnery Schools. Three, Nos. 2, 11 and 12, based respectively at Dalcross, Andreas and Bishops Court, received several Mk.VIIs. More than 30 Spitfire Mk.VIIs were flown by the AGSs, eventhough 12 AGS was disbanded on 31 May 1945. No. 2 AGS followed in November and only No.11 AGS continued to use some Mk.VIIs until 1947. The usage of the Spitfire Mk.VII was not, of course, accident free. No. 2 AGS lost one aircraft on 20 April 1945 after an engine failure. The pilot made a forced-landing on the beach at Cape Wrath without injury. A second aircraft was lost on 6 June owing to engine trouble. The pilot made a wheels-up landing. No.11 AGS lost two aircraft. The first was on 11 October 1945, when an engine failure during take-off required an emergency landing near Andreas. The pilot was slightly injured. One month later P/O Eric G. Gale was killed carrying out a dummy attack on a Wellington. A handful of Mk.VIIs were also used by miscellaneous units, mainly as a hack or communication aircraft, by the end of the war and into the post-war period. A couple were lost in various accidents, none concerning second line units, during ferry flights (like MD115 which overshot at Catterick or MB912 which swung on take-off and hit a floodlight at Hawarden). MD178 was lost while being ferried by No.1 Aircraft Delivery Flight.

Date	Pilot	S/N	Origin	Serial	Code	Unit	Fate
17.02.44	S/O P.M. **Lynch**	-	ATA	**MD115**		7 FP	-
10.02.45	T/O H. **Prince**	-	ATA	**MB912**		3 FP	-
01.03.45	F/O Edwards **Robins**	NZ415784	RNZAF	**MD178**		1 ADF	-
20.04.45	P/O John B. **Todd**	RAF No. 191309	RAF	**MD109**		2 AGS	-
06.06.45	F/O Henry G. **Vickery**	RAF No. 163989	RAF	**MD100**		2 AGS	-
10.06.45	P/O John C. **Steele**	RAF No. 150198	RAF	**MD180**	W	519 Sqn	-
11.10.45	W/O John T. **Gordon**	RAF No. 1671461	RAF	**MD169**		11 AGS	-
07.11.45	F/Sgt William A. **Sperry**	RAF No. 1194831	RAF	**EN506**	V	519 Sqn	-
09.11.45	P/O Eric G. **Gale**	RAF No. 200767	RAF	**MD112**		11 AGS	†

One of the few Mk.VIIs issued to a Meteorological unit, MD159, flying with No.1402 Flight at the end of summer 1944 before the Flight was absorbed into No.518 Sqn. Note the absence of guns, totally useless for the weather flights the Mk.VII had to carry out.

Side view and close up of MD159 in flight. The pointed wings tips were still necessary as the weather Mk.VIIs flew at high altitude. At the time, most surviving Mk.VIIs are believed to have had them removed and replaced by rounded wing tips.

Simplified register

Serial	month of delivery	Squadron
BS121	Sep.42	**124** *(ON-A)*
BS142	Sep.42	**124** *(ON-H)*
BS229	Nov.42	-
BS253	Oct.42	**616**
EN178	Dec.42	-
EN192	Dec.42	**124**
EN285	Dec.42	**124** *(ON-Y)*
EN297	Dec.42	**519**
EN310	Jan.43	**124** *(ON-R)*
EN457	Jan.43	**124** *(ON-C)*
EN465	Feb.43	**131**
EN470	Feb.43	-
EN474	Mar.43	-
EN477	Feb.43	**616**
EN494	Apr.43	**616**
EN495	Mar.43	**124** *(ON-E)*, **131**
EN496	Apr.43	**124** *(ON-U)*
EN497	Apr.43	**124** *(ON-P)*
EN499	Apr.43	**124** *(ON-D)*, **131**
EN505	May.43	**124** *(ON-S)*
EN506	Jul.43	**124**, **519** *(V)*
EN509	May.43	**124** *(ON-G)*
EN511	May.43	**124** *(ON-F)*
EN512	May.43	**124** *(ON-N)*
MB761	Jul.43	**124** *(ON-G)*, **1402 Flt**
MB762	Jul.43	**616**
MB763	Jul.43	**312, 118, 453**
MB764	Jul.43	**616**
MB765	Aug.43	**312, 118, 453**
MB766	Aug.43	**124**
MB767	Aug.43	**616** *(YQ-F)*
MB768	Aug.43	**616** *(YQ-X)*
MB769	Aug.43	**616** *(YQ-T)*
MB806	May.43	**124** *(ON-X)*
MB808	May.43	**124** *(ON-C)*, **616** *(YQ-F)*
MB820	May.43	**124** *(ON-E)*
MB821	May.43	**124** *(ON-U)*
MB822	Jun.43	**124** *(ON-L)*, **616**
MB823	Jun.43	**124** *(ON-T)*
MB824	Jun.43	**124** *(ON-Z)*, **616**
MB825	Jun.43	**124** *(ON-D)*, **616** *(YQ-P)*
MB826	Jun.43	**124** *(ON-J)*
MB827	Jun.43	**124** *(ON-U)*
MB828	Jun.43	**312, 118, 453**
MB883	Jan.44	**131**
MB884	Feb.44	**131**
MB885	Feb.44	**616** *(YQ-V)*
MB886	Feb.44	**124**
MB887	Feb.44	**131**
MB912	Sep.43	**124, 1402 Flt**
MB913	Sep.43	**616** *(YQ-G)*
MB914	Sep.43	**616**
MB915	Sep.43	**616**

MB916	Sep.43	**124** *(ON-N)*
MB929	Oct.43	**616** *(YQ-J)*
MB930	Oct.43	**616** *(YQ-R)*
MB931	Oct.43	**131, 19**
MB932	Feb.44	**131**
MB933	Feb.44	-
MB934	Feb.44	**616**
MB935	Feb.44	**131** *(NX-Z)*
MD100	Nov.43	**616**
MD101	Nov.43	**616** *(YQ-C)*
MD102	Nov.43	**616, 303**
MD103	Nov.43	-
MD104	Nov.43	**616** *(YQ-R)*
MD105	Nov.43	**616**
MD106	Dec.43	**616** *(YQ-W)*
MD107	Dec.43	**616**
MD108	Dec.43	**616** *(YQ-E)*
MD109	Dec.43	-
MD110	Dec.43	**131**
MD111	Dec.43	**131** *(NX-Q)*, **154** *(HG-Q)*
MD112	Dec.43	**124** *(ON-F)*
MD113	Dec.43	**124**
MD114	Dec.43	-
MD115	Dec.43	-
MD116	Dec.43	**616, 131, 616** *(YQ-K)*
MD117	Dec.43	**131**
MD118	Dec.43	-
MD119	Dec.43	**131**
MD120	Dec.43	**131** *(NX-O)*, **154**
MD121	Jan.44	**616**
MD122	Jan.44	-
MD123	Jan.44	**131**
MD124	Jan.44	**131**
MD125	Jan.44	**131** *(NX-X)*
MD126	Jan.44	**124**
MD127	Jan.44	**124**
MD128	Jan.44	**131**
MD129	Feb.44	**131, 154**
MD130	Jan.44	**124, 1402 Flt, 518**
MD131	Jan.44	**131**
MD132	Jan.44	**131, 154**
MD133	Jan.44	**616**
MD134	Jan.44	**131** *(NX-P)*, **154**
MD135	Jan.44	**124**
MD136	Jan.44	**131**
MD137	Jan.44	**616, 131, 616**
MD138	Jan.44	-
MD139	Jan.44	**124** *(ON-W)*
MD140	Jan.44	**616**
MD141	Feb.44	**519**
MD142	Jan.44	-
MD143	Feb.44	**131, 154**
MD144	Feb.44	**131, 154**
MD145	Feb.44	**124**
MD146	Feb.44	**131, 154**
MD159	Feb.44	**131, 616, 1402 Flt, 519** *(B)*
MD160	Feb.44	**131**
MD161	Mar.44	**124**
MD162	Mar.44	**124**
MD163	Mar.44	**124**

MD164	Mar.44	**124** *(ON-P)*
MD165	Mar.44	**131** *(NX-M)*, **154**
MD166	Jan.44	**131**
MD167	Mar.44	**124**
MD168	Mar.44	**124, 154** *(HG-Y)*
MD169	Mar.44	**131, 154**
MD170	Mar.44	**131, 154**
MD171	Mar.44	**131**
MD172	Mar.44	**131** *(NX-L)*
MD173	Mar.44	**131, 154**
MD174	Mar.44	**616, 131, 154**
MD175	Mar.44	-
MD176	Mar.44	-
MD177	Apr.44	**616**
MD178	Apr.44	**616** *(YQ-W)*, **131, 154**
MD179	Apr.44	**124**
MD180	Apr.44	**519** *(W)*
MD181	May.44	**616, 1402 Flt, 518**
MD182	Apr.44	**616** *(YQ-E)*
MD183	Apr.44	**131, 154**
MD184	May.44	**124**
MD185	May.44	**131, 154** *(HG-U)*
MD186	May.44	**131, 154**
MD187	May.44	**131** *(NX-V)*, **154**
MD188	May.44	**131**
MD189	May.44	**616**
MD190	May.44	-

Desmond P. Kelly of No. 124 Squadron posing in front of a Spitfire VII. An Australian from Victoria he joined 124 in late spring 1943 and flew initially on Spitfire Mk VI. He was later posted to No. 616 Squadron and lost an eye in combat. He tried to return on operations after recovery but was unsuccessful. However, ironically, Kelly was one of the first Australian pilot to fly the Meteor and became a conversion pilot on 1330 CU. (*Brendan Kelly via Drew Harrison*)

✝

IN MEMORIAM
Spitfire Mk.VII

Name	Service No	Rank	Age	Origin	Date	Serial
ALLEN, Victor Jack Trafford	RAF No. 1579427	Sgt	19	RAF	29.06.44	MB762
ATKINSON, William James	AUS. 413332	W/O	21	RAAF	01.06.44	MB887
BEARMAN, Cecil Ernest	RAF No. 122343	F/L	27	RAF	25.08.44	MD171
GALE, Eric Gordon	RAF No. 200767	P/O	27	RAF	09.11.45	MD112
GORDON, Walter	RAF No. 1016772	Sgt	21	RAF	05.11.43	MB929
HARRISON, Geoffrey Austin	RAF No. 60102	F/L	n/k	RAF	12.06.44	MD121
HART, Robert Arthur	AUS. 408257	W/O	21	RAAF	19.06.44	MD133
HURST, Albert Harding	RAF No. 150381	F/O	n/k	RAF	14.01.45	MD165
JOHNSTON, Donald Edward	AUS. 412550	F/Sgt	21	RAAF	01.04.44	MD116
MOODY, Vincent Kenneth	CAN./ J.15362	F/L	24	RCAF	12.06.44	MD123
PHELPS, Eric John	RAF No. 1291762	F/Sgt	22	RAF	14.05.43	EN496
PHILIPPS, Douglas Frederick*	AUS. 401394	W/O	25	RAAF	24.04.44	MB935
PROUTING, George Edward	RAF No. 175505	P/O	22	RAF	22.05.44	MD108
RUTHERFORD, Frank Wallace	RAF No. 1497152	F/Sgt	22	RAF	03.12.43	MB930
WOODEY, Jack Edward	AUS. 411625	W/O	24	RAAF	07.06.44	MB883

Total: 15

Australia: 5, Canada: 1, United Kingdom: 9

*Irish-born Australian

n/k: Not known

Supermarine Spitfire Mk. VII EN285
No. 124 (Baroda) Squadron
Flight Sergeant Desmond P. 'Ned' KELLY (RAAF)
Northolt (UK), summer 1943

Supermarine Spitfire Mk. VII EN509
No. 124 (Baroda) Squadron
Bradwell Bay (UK), summmer 1944

Supermarine Spitfire Mk. VII MD120
No. 131 (County of Kent) Squadron
Squadron Leader James J. 'Orange' O'MEARA
Culmhead (UK), March 1944

Supermarine Spitfire Mk. VII MD111
No. 131 (County of Kent) Squadron
Culmhead (UK), summer 1944

Supermarine Spitfire Mk. VII MD111
No. 154 Squadron
Biggin Hill (UK), winter 1944-1945

Supermarine Spitfire Mk. VII MD182
No. 616 Squadron
Flight Lieutenant Jack Mc. CLELAND (RNZAF)
Manston (UK), September 1944

SQUADRONS! - The series

1. The Supermarine Spitfire Mk VI
2. The Republic Thunderbolt Mk I
3. The Supermarine Spitfire Mk V in the Far East
4. The Boeing Fortress Mk I
5. The Supermarine Spitfire Mk XII
6. The Supermarine Spitfire Mk VII
7. The Supermarine Spitfire F. 21
8. The Handley-Page Halifax Mk I
9. The Forgotten Fighters
10. The NA Mustang IV in Western Europe
11. The NA Mustang IV over the Balkans and Italy
12. The Supermarine Spitfire Mk XVI - *The British*
13. The Martin Marauder Mk I
14. The Supermarine Spitfire Mk VIII in the Southwest Pacific - *The British*
15. The Gloster Meteor F.I & F.III
16. The NA Mitchell - *The Dutch, Poles and French*
17. The Curtiss Mohawk
18. The Curtiss Kittyhawk Mk II
19. The Boulton Paul Defiant - *day and night fighter*
20. The Supermarine Spitfire Mk VIII in the Southwest Pacific - *The Australians*
21. The Boeing Fortress Mk II & Mk III
22. The Douglas Boston and Havoc - *The Australians*
23. The Republic Thunderbolt Mk II
24. The Douglas Boston and Havoc - *Night fighters*
25. The Supermarine Spitfire Mk V - *The Eagles*
26. The Hawker Hurricane - *The Canadians*
27. The Supermarine Spitfire Mk V - *The 'Bombay' squadrons*
28. The Consolidated Liberator - *The Australians*
29. The Supermarine Spitfire Mk XVI - *The Dominions*
30. The Supermarine Spitfire Mk V - *The Belgian and Dutch squadrons*
31. The Supermarine Spitfire Mk V - *The New-Zealanders*
32. The Supermarine Spitfire Mk V - *The Norwegians*
33. The Brewster Buffalo
34. The Supermarine Spitfire Mk II - *The Foreign squadrons*
35. The Martin Marauder Mk II
36. The Supermarine Spitfire Mk V - *The Special Reserve squadrons*
37. The Supermarine Spitfire Mk XIV - *The Belgian and Dutch squadrons*
38. The Supermarine Spitfire Mk II - *The Rhodesian, Dominion & Eagle squadrons*
39. The Douglas Boston and Havoc - *Intruders*
40. The North American Mustang Mk III over Italy and the Balkans (Pt-1)
41. The Bristol Brigand
42. The Supermarine Spitfire Mk V - *The Australians*
43. The Hawker Typhoon - *The Rhodesian squadrons*
44. The Supermarine Spitfire F.22 & F.24
45. The Supermarine Spitfire Mk IX - *The Belgian and Dutch squadrons*
46. The North American & CAC Mustang - *The RAAF*
47. The Westland Whirlwind
48. The Supermarine Spitfire Mk XIV - *The British squadrons*
49. The Supermarine Spitfire Mk I - *The beginning (the Auxiliary squadrons)*
50. The Hawker Tempest Mk V - *The New Zealanders*
51. The Last of the Long-Range Biplane Flying Boats
52. The Supermarine Spitfire Mk IX - *The Former Canadian Homefront squadrons*
53. The Hawker Hurricane Mk I & Mk II - *The Eagle squadrons*
54. The Hawker biplane fighters
55. The Supermarine Spitfire Mk IX - *The Auxiliary squadrons*
56. The Hawker Typhoon - *The Canadian squadrons*
57. The Douglas SBD - *New Zealand and France*
58. The Forgotten Patrol Seaplanes
59. The Dutch Fighter Squadrons - *Nos. 322 & 120 (NEI) Squadrons*
60. The Supermarine Spitfire - *The Australian Squadrons in Western Europe and the Med*
61. The Belgian Fighter Squadrons - *Nos. 349 & 350 Squadrons*
62. The Supermarine Spitfire Mk I - *The beginning (the Regular squadrons)*
63. The Hawker Typhoon - *The 'Fellowship of the Bellows' squadrons*
64. The North American Mustang Mk I & Mk II

Introducing's RAF In Combat and Bravo Bravo Aviation's collection of highly-detailed and historically accurate, high-quality aviation prints. For more information on available prints, please visit:

 or

Prints available for this book:

PL-027: J.J. O'Meara
PL-183: L.W. Watts
PL-184: T. Balmforth

www.ingramcontent.com/pod-product-compliance
Lightning Source LLC
Chambersburg PA
CBHW060822090426
42738CB00002B/78